RUMRUNNING

in

SUFFOLK COUNTY

RUMRUNNING
in
SUFFOLK COUNTY

Tales from Liquor Island

A M Y K A S U G A F O L K

THE
History
PRESS

Published by The History Press
Charleston, SC
www.historypress.com

Copyright © 2022 by Amy Kasuga Folk
All rights reserved

First published 2022

Manufactured in the United States

ISBN 9781467151610

Library of Congress Control Number: 2022933368

Notice: The information in this book is true and complete to the best of our knowledge. It is offered without guarantee on the part of the author or The History Press. The author and The History Press disclaim all liability in connection with the use of this book.

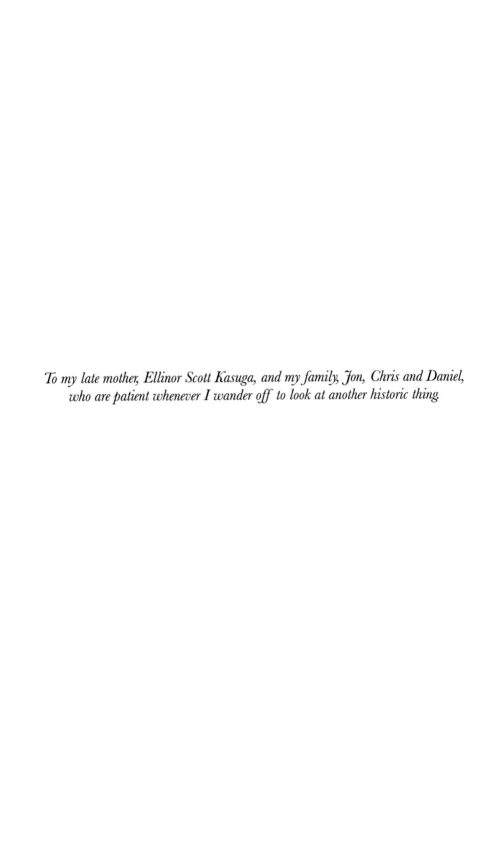

To my late mother, Ellinor Scott Kasuga, and my family, Jon, Chris and Daniel, who are patient whenever I wander off to look at another historic thing.

CONTENTS

ACKNOWLEDGEMENTS

My thanks to the Oysterponds Historical Society; Southold Historical Museum; Pierce Rafferty and the Henry L. Ferguson Museum; Mary Casone, the Town of Babylon historian; Julie Greene, the Town of Southampton historian; Barbara Russell, the Town of Brookhaven historian; Stephen San Fillipo; the Quogue Historical Society; Andrea Meyer of the East Hampton Public Library; and Herb Strobel and Richard Wines of Hallockville Museum Farm.

INTRODUCTION

Stories about rumrunning abound across Long Island. Each waterfront community has local tales of Prohibition and the excitement and daring of the men who transported alcohol from large ships outside U.S. territorial waters to the winding shores of the island and passed the shipments to the bootleggers who would drive the load to its destination. Most of the stories that abounded locally are about rumrunning involving unnamed local residents sneaking alcohol in from the offshore boats. The stories, with an appropriate amount of excitement, usually involved outwitting the authorities. What happened to the liquor after it came ashore was never really specified, except some said, "Well of course it went to the local restaurants or bars." The reality of the rumrunning business was a lot darker than local memory paints it.

As odd as it sounds to our modern ears today, from early in history, humankind realized that drinking water was, at times, really dangerous. Undetectable hazards such as bacteria could lurk in local wells, waiting for a chance to sicken those who drank from them. Liquor, on the other hand, in moderation, was not nearly as hazardous.

The earliest evidence of alcohol being made can be found in Egyptian tombs from the Old Kingdom. Some Egyptians, wanting to make sure they had a steady supply of everything they needed in the afterlife, including beer, had "magical" servants called *shabti*, and among these servants were brewers.[1]

Model of brewers and bakers from an Egyptian tomb, 1981–1975 BC, Middle Kingdom, on display at the Metropolitan Museum of Art in New York City. *Author's collection.*

Since the process of making alcohol kills bacteria, throughout history, men, women and children commonly drank mildly alcoholic beverages such as small beer, which is equivalent to some of our modern light beers. Drinking was so ingrained in society that one of the earliest functions of a grocery store was as a saloon.[2] Many storeowners capitalized on the social function of their enterprise by providing alcoholic and nonalcoholic beverages for sale by the bottle for home consumption or by the glass for immediate gratification.[3]

During the nineteenth century, Americans differentiated between wine, beer and all other alcoholic beverages. Small beer and wine regularly drunk as a part of an adult's daily routine were regarded as benign. Other forms of alcohol, such as rum and brandy, were considered intoxicants.[4] By the 1830s, drinking was a well-established social ritual, and the average adult in the United States consumed between four and seven gallons of alcohol per year. By comparison, in the 1970s, the average adult consumed only approximately two and a half gallons per year.[5]

Although Americans were a pretty hard-drinking culture, temperance crusaders like Neal Dow of Maine began to add biased language against new immigrants—such as the Irish Catholic refugees from the potato famine— into their speeches. In the nineteenth century, nativist prejudice linked the new arrivals with drunkenness. Dow, who was a popular temperance speaker, perceived the influx of immigrants as "given to lower-class indulgences and disgracefully lax in family disciplines....The more immigration increased, the more hostile he became to foreigners."[6] Citizens across the country prodded by this rhetoric began to fear what was seen as the foreign, alcohol-swilling masses flooding into the country.

Many feared that these newcomers to the United States would not only take away jobs but also drink their wages away and abandon the welfare of their large families to hardworking Americans. It was thought that the foreign attitudes toward drinking would also infect the innocent young men of this country and we would end up with a nation of drunkards.[7]

These fears were mixed in with the sermons of ministers exhorting their congregations that drinking led to a moral decline, poverty and damaged health.[8] This mixture of fears threw support to not only the temperance movement but also anti-immigration organizations.

In 1825, Currier and Ives came out with a print called *The Drunkard's Progress*, which stated,

> *A drunkard is the annoyance of modesty; the trouble of civility; the spoil of wealth; the distraction of reason; he is only the brewer's agent: the tavern*

and ale-house benefactor. The beggar's companion; the constable's trouble; he is his wife's woe, his children's sorrow; his neighbor's scoff; his own shame; in summer, he is a tub of swill; a spirit of sleep; a picture of beast, and a monster of a man.[9]

In Southold Town, this message resonated with the people of Oysterponds Lower Neck, today known as Orient. Led by the local Congregational minister, the Oysterponds and Sterling Temperance Society began and quickly spread throughout the community in 1829.[10]

While the temperance movement started in the 1820s, it wasn't until the 1860s, during the Civil War, that the movement really began to gain popular support. In the following decade, movements like the National Christian Temperance Union, the Woman's Christian Temperance Union, and the Washingtonian–Sons of Temperance swelled across the nation and took hold to varying degrees in local communities.

Despite their names, temperance organizations' goal was to not temper or limit the use of alcohol but to prohibit it. While the Eighteenth Amendment to the U.S. Constitution prohibited the production, sale and transport of "intoxicating liquors," it did not define what was an intoxicating liquor or provide penalties. The amendment gave the government the power to enforce the ban by "appropriate legislation."[11]

By 1917, America had been drawn into World War I, and temperance supporters in Congress managed to insert language into an agricultural bill to ban the sale of liquor to soldiers. In 1919, at the conclusion of the war, a bill to ban the sale of alcohol was introduced and passed in Congress.[12]

The bill, which the Anti-Saloon League helped to write, was named for Andrew Volstead of Minnesota, chairman of the House Judiciary Committee. The Volstead Act was created to carry out the intent of the Eighteenth Amendment and established Prohibition. Enacted in 1920, the bill—while supported by many temperance members—posed a problem for the rest of society.

Andrew Volstead of Minnesota, chairman of the House Judiciary Committee. The act that started Prohibition was named after him. *Library of Congress.*

PROHIBITION

When you think about the Roaring Twenties in comparison to the decades before it, the 1920s was a major revolution. Skirts shortened; women's hairstyles shortened; and attitudes about relationships and what could and could not be done in public altered. Society began to change radically. Those changes set the tone for our society today.

For the first year, most people regarded Prohibition as an inconvenience. Businesses that served alcohol had to either change their work models, or in some cases, clubs and wealthy people who had stored a large supply of liquor in bonded warehouses could technically, according to the law, continue drinking from their supplies until they ran out.[13] Medical exemptions were offered for patients whom doctors determined alcohol would help their overall health—but the government monitored the number of these exemptions that were given out.[14] Only a drink known as near beer and wine that had an alcoholic content of 2.75 percent remained legal.

People in the United States began to get very thirsty. A number of people began to make booze in their homes for personal consumption. Others saw bigger, more commercial ways to cater to this growing thirst, and a cat-and-mouse game began between the government and those supplying liquor to owners of a new type of business—the speakeasy—also known locally as "blind tigers."

In the 1920s, the United States imported most hard liquor from Canada, Bermuda, Scotland and France as well as a number of other countries. Understandably, Prohibition affected not only America but also the international beverage industry. Businessmen seeing the new but rapidly

If you had a heart condition, your doctor could prescribe a shot of booze for your health. However, the business was tightly regulated. *Courtesy of the Southold Historical Museum, Southold, New York.*

growing market set about filling the need. At first, it was relatively easy to smuggle in a crate or two. Then the government created the Prohibition unit and tasked the Department of the Treasury to work with the Coast Guard to enforce the law.[15]

Events then started to take a darker turn. One of the laws of business states that where there is a need, someone is going to step up to fill that need—and make a buck. Prior to Prohibition, New York City's criminal element consisted of what you could call bullies and toughs—basically street gangs that ruled over their own small neighborhoods.[16] Prohibition changed all that.

ARNOLD ROTHSTEIN WAS "THE black sheep of a wealthy German Jewish family from the upper West-side."[17] As a teenager, he worked as a translator for immigrants and New York City's Tammany Hall bosses. A gambler, the thirty-eight-year-old Rothstein soon saw the need created by Prohibition. He provided the financing for several gangs to purchase and "import" ships of booze. His crews not only organized ships to anchor off Long Island's shores but also gathered drivers and vehicles to ship the crates up to the city.[18] While it still sounds like a bit like a lark ducking the law, these gangs were deadly serious about this business venture. Thousands of dollars changed hands with each shipment.

To give you an idea of how big of a business this was, the gang on average paid $200 a week to one hundred employees when the average store clerk took home $25 a week, and they paid $100,000 a week in graft to police, federal agents and city and court officials. Despite these expenses, the gang still took in an estimated net profit of $12 million a year from the business.[19]

Arthur Simon Flegenheimer, better known as Dutch Schultz, was born in New York City in 1902. Schultz, like Rothstein, came from a German

When Americans started to get thirsty, crime figures such as Dutch Schultz stepped in to supply liquor for a price. *Library of Congress.*

Jewish background. Schultz had a violent temper and made his fortune in organized crime—particularly bootlegging and the numbers racket. Starting in the Bronx as small-time hoodlum, Schultz was involved in a war for control of the city's beer supply and took over control of the importation of booze from Long Island.[20]

Irving "Waxy" Gordon, Jacob "Little Augie" Orgen, Jack "Legs" Diamond, Salvatore Lucania (also known as Charles "Lucky" Luciano), Maier Suchowljansky (better known as Meyer Lansky), Francesco Castiglia (better known as Frank Costello), Joe Adonis, Vannie Higgins and Benjamin "Bugsy" Siegel were also part of this group of importers. Long Island only missed having Al Capone involved in the area because he moved from New York City to Chicago the year before Prohibition started. Eventually, these gangs evolved into the criminal enterprises we now know as the Italian, Jewish and Irish mafias.[21]

HOW DID THE RUMRUNNING BUSINESS WORK?

In the rumrunning business, groups of investors from both sides of the ocean would buy shiploads of liquor. The cargo would either be delivered to a specific customer, or it was offered for sale to anyone approaching the ship. Sometimes the load would be a mixture of alcohol intended for a specific destination with extra cases for the spur-of-the-moment customer that approached the vessel.[22]

The ships with their banned cargo would anchor outside the territorial waters of the United States, which in 1920 was three miles off the coast. Later, in 1924, in an effort to make rumrunning more difficult, the United States moved the line to twelve miles away from the coast.[23] The line of ships hovering just outside the United States' border was nicknamed Rum Row.[24] Small, fast boats would go out to the larger boats to pick up or purchase crates of liquor and then race back to shore—while avoiding the notice of the Coast Guard. Once on shore, the cargo was transferred to either a vehicle for transport to its final destination or was hidden locally until it was safe to move.

The business of importing liquor was very organized; rumrunners soon began to use the airwaves and shortwave radios to arrange their deals. Coded messages detailing inventory, orders, sales and other details of the business were broadcasted.[25] Likewise messages between coordinating pickups and landings of the various rumrunners were broadcasted. At one point, "Radio became useful to the syndicates when the offshore rum vessels began sending daily code messages through a commercial radio station addressed

Often a clandestine meeting during the dark of night, a rumrunner under sail rendezvoused with a larger ship to get a cargo of liquor. *Library of Congress.*

to their representatives."[26] In and around Long Island, shortwave radios sent coded messages arranging sales and transportation details.[27] In 1925, the federal government created a team to monitor the airwaves for messages. Then, beginning in 1926, a cryptological team was started to try to break the codes.[28] Coast Guard cryptologists, particularly Elizebeth S. Friedman, broke most of the rumrunners' codes by 1927.[29]

The process of rumrunning was simple and easy to romanticize, especially since gangs weren't the only ones importing from overseas. However, this was a lucrative business that attracted some unsavory people. The anchored ships of Rum Row were periodically boarded by pirates who would rob and then kill everyone on board.[30] While on shore, organized gangs like Dutch Schultz's hijacked, terrorized or killed anyone whose vehicle they suspected to be transporting any significant quantity of booze into the city.[31] That was just on the criminal side.

The federal government was, in some instances, just a violent as the gangs. It authorized officers to stop, search and detain anyone they suspected of violating the Volstead Act. The Prohibition unit, which was first an arm of the Treasury Department and later became part of the

Justice Department, along with the Coast Guard, was authorized to use deadly force to carry out the Volstead Act.[32] It is estimated that nationwide more than one hundred innocent bystanders died in the enforcement of the act.[33] In addition, federal law rendered these officers untouchable from prosecution because they were acting in the course of their jobs.

There are a number of local stories about rumrunners working in Suffolk County—from people finding suitcases with bottles of alcohol in their garage as a thank-you gift for ignoring rumrunner and bootlegger activities to active participation in the smuggling.

On April 7, 1933, it was all over. Many historians credit Nelson Rockefeller with swaying public opinion enough to have politicians repeal Prohibition.[34] The Grand Experiment was done, and many citizens across the United States breathed a sigh of relief.

1921

Local stories about rumrunning probably exist in every shoreline community across Long Island. While some stories were published in the newspapers, many more were related locally. Few names if any were attached to the stories because of the less than legal nature of rumrunning. Although the events happened barely one hundred years ago, gathering information on the topic is difficult at best. Many of those who were involved in the business were reluctant, even after the end of Prohibition, to talk to historians, fearing retroactive prosecution because trafficking in liquor had been illegal and the repercussions had been severe.

Sure that the rumrunning and bootlegging business was widespread on the East End, federal judge Edwin L. Garvin needed someone he trusted to investigate the latest case of liquor smuggling. Garvin handpicked Assistant U.S. Attorney Francis A. McGurk to take charge of the investigation into the activities of the recently captured schooner *Henry L. Marshall*.

The ship was stopped off New Jersey and found to be carrying cases of liquor destined for thirsty inhabitants. McGurk declared to the newspapers that he was sure that the case was somehow connected to the East End of Long Island. He swore that he was going to question residents of Montauk Point, Greenport and Sag Harbor, sure that some of the residents of those areas were involved in bootlegging.[35]

On a quiet Sunday morning in Huntington on a road close to Jericho Turnpike, U.S. Attorney Wallace E.J Collins and U.S. Marshal James M. Powers—along with twelve deputy marshals, all armed—waited in hushed anticipation to see if their tip paid off. Streams of illegal booze had been finding their way into the hotels and roadhouses of the town, although nary a truck had been seen delivering to any of the establishments.

Soon the sound of a powerful engine was heard approaching, breaking the hush of the morning, and a touring car with six men was spotted. As the car drew level with the waiting men, they leaped out into the road, stopping the car. The marshals quickly surrounded the vehicle and subdued the passengers. The interior of the car was crammed with twenty-five cases of whiskey.

The bootleggers were trying a new strategy, abandoning the heavy trucks in favor of blending in with cars in the heavy traffic on Long Island's roadways.

1922

William J. Hunt, a motorcycle traffic officer for the town of Islip, had a dilemma. He stood to make a lot of money; the catch was, he didn't have a fast boat. But he knew who did. Hunt approached the captain of the powerboat *Joe Bill* with a business offer.

Hunt's friends were anxious to have someone move 1,495 cases of liquor from a transport ship anchored twenty-six miles offshore. The five men Hunt introduced to Christopher Locker were so anxious to get their cargo moved that they were willing to pay Locker $5,000 for the trip.

Unbeknownst to Hunt or his friends, Locker was allied with a newly hired local Prohibition agent, Isabel Premm, who was hired by the government for her zeal and contacts in the community. Shortly after receiving the job offer, Locker was swearing out a statement about the meeting to the district attorney and fingering the men.

Locker and his powerboat were regularly hired by the feds to patrol the waters of the bay and Fire Island Inlet looking for rumrunners. Only a week earlier, Premm and Locker were part of the operation that caught the sloop *Virginia* with five hundred cases of contraband.[36]

TIPPED OFF BY AN anonymous phone call, New York State troopers stationed in Bay Shore took to the water in November 1922. The officers were told that a rumrunner was planning to land its cargo in the middle of the night as the community slept.

3218　　THE CREEK AT BREWSTER'S DOCK, BAY SHORE, L. I.　　ILLUSTRATED POST CARD CO., N. Y.

The many small inlets of Long Island provided a number of docking places for rumrunners. *Courtesy of the Oysterponds Historical Society, Orient, New York.*

Arriving in the nick of time to find a truck leaving the dock, the officers pulled over Charles Crampe, a local taxi driver, driving a truck that was loaded with one hundred cases of high-grade alcohol estimated to be worth $12,000 and slated to be delivered to the city.

After learning that the ship that unloaded the crates was close by, the officers piled into a motorboat and headed out onto the still waters of Brightwaters Bay. They chased the rumrunning sloop several miles before finally overtaking the ship and arresting the crew.[37]

———

BRUNO STEPHANOWITZ LIVED NEAR a nice, quiet place, the Riverhead Cemetery. One night in waning days of summer, there must have been a whiff of something in the air that led Officer W. Arthur Nugent to discover Stephanowitz using a large still. As Stephanowitz sat in his jail cell awaiting his trial, he worried about his house and its contents. He was apparently unaware that all communications into and out of the jail were monitored by authorities. So driven by his worries Bruno wrote to his brother that he needed him to move to his house while he was in jail. Also, he included in the letter the warning to be sure to stay away from the barrel of whiskey that he had made—because it was still aging. Additionally, Stephanowitz worried that someone might have put poison in the whiskey barrel during his absence.

During the trial, Bruno Stephanowitz protested that the situation was not as it appeared. He was using the still to create distilled water for his car. The officer countered this excuse: Stephanowitz was caught with not only the still but also whiskey mash and a quantity of liquor in his possession. Then the letter, which never made it to his brother, was brought out as evidence. This left Stephanowitz facing two additional indictments in court and a very real need for his brother to take care of his house.[38]

JUDGE GEORGE H. FURMAN was working overtime and into the night because of the number of cases brought before his bench in the late fall of 1922. Among those cases was William Gray, alias William Franklin of Manhattan. Gray was brought before the county court in Riverhead on charges of transporting liquor. He was arrested in Bay Shore with a jug under his arm, openly selling hooch as he worked his way down the street—until he offered a quick drink to Probation Officer Charles J. Odell, who was walking down the street on business.[39]

Also appearing in front of Judge Furman were Alexander and Petronella Sataneck of Sagaponack. Instead of taking part in the importing of intoxicating liquor, the couple decided to make and sell it themselves. Walter Kassett of East Hampton, whose case followed the Satanecks, also pleaded guilty to possessing intoxicating liquors. In both cases, the accused were sentenced to steep fines.[40]

1923

One of the first mentions of rumrunning in the town of Southold to appear in the newspaper was this story from Arshamomaque.

Sheriff Amza W. Biggs was a dedicated lawman. A resident of Huntington, Biggs became fascinated with law enforcement when he got to know the local sheriff, who rented horses and carriages from young Biggs's livery stable. By 1908, Biggs had decided to change careers; he sold off his stable and joined local law enforcement as a deputy sheriff.[41] Pursuing his new career with great enthusiasm, Biggs quickly made a name for himself, catching criminals and solving crimes in the area. Becoming active in the local Republican Party, Biggs, a popular candidate, ran for and won the sheriff's election in 1916 and again in 1923.[42]

On, Sunday, June 17, 1923, Biggs learned that a boatload of whiskey had been landed on the dock in Greenport at two o'clock in the morning. The tip made no mention of where the booze had been stashed while awaiting transport.

That same night, Sidney Smith of Greenport, unable to sleep, went out for a late-night stroll, enjoying the peace down by the docks and railroad station. As he was passing the property of fisherman Captain Fred Davis, he saw a woman going into the house. The door soon opened again, and an unfriendly Davis appeared with a shotgun and fired at Smith, striking him in the face and ear with shotgun pellets. Injured and aggrieved, Smith notified Sheriff Biggs of the incident. A warrant was quickly issued, and Biggs assigned a group of deputies to begin observing the property.

For Sheriff
AMZA W.
BIGGS

Amza Wetmore
Biggs Jr. (1904–1957)
spent thirty years in
law enforcement as
county sheriff and
later as Huntington's
police chief. *From
the* Long Islander,
*October 13, 1916,
page 7.*

After a short while, the deputies spotted Ernest Martin of Hempstead, John Monahan and William Kalbacert of Greenport driving an Eastern Auto Supply Company truck off the Davis property. When the truck was stopped by the deputies, it was found to be filled with crates of liquor. Biggs suspected that the truck had only a portion of the haul that was landed at the dock and continued to have his men watch the property.

The next evening, an estimated sixty to seventy professional New York gunmen heavily armed arrived at Fred Davis's house. The newcomers faced down the eight deputy sheriffs, who were powerless to prevent the removal of approximately six hundred cases of scotch and rye whiskey from the barn on the property.[43]

CLARENCE DOWNS OF SAG Harbor and a group of friend narrowly escaped death when gunmen protecting a gang of bootleggers and rumrunners confronted Downs and his friends. The group was heading home from a visit to Montauk when the driver made a wrong turn on to Devon Road and headed down toward the beach in Amagansett. As soon as they noticed their mistake and were looking for a place to turn around, Downs and his friends realized they were in a really bad place. A group of men with guns soon spotted them and began to brandish their weapons. When one of the gunmen leaped onto the running board of the car and began to smash at the window, the men thought they might never see another sunrise again.

The driver hastily backed out, turned around and raced the car back down the road toward Montauk Highway. But leaving was not good enough; the gunmen leaped into a "high powered Marmon car" and followed, shooting at the fleeing automobile. When the car carrying Downs reached the turn off, they tried to take the turn at a high rate of speed and flipped their auto three times before finally coming to rest. Although the car was demolished, the occupants had only minor injuries. After witnessing the accident, the gunmen probably assumed the passengers were dead, turned around and returned to their posts. Locals noted that seven large trucks loaded with liquor left various points in East Hampton,

6069   MAIN STREET, Amagansett. L. I.

One of the communities on the far east end, Amagansett was a quiet place when the sun was up during Prohibition. *Courtesy of the Oysterponds Historical Society, Orient, New York.*

each heading toward the city. The trucks were escorted by several cars carrying armed guards.[44]

———❧———

ISABEL PREMM OF BAY Shore was only twenty-one years old when she applied to become a Prohibition agent. In a newspaper interview, she said,

> *I do many things—keep track of boats going in and out of different inlets. I skirt the shore line at night in my motorcar and I have kept a sharp watch on seamen who I knew could pilot a boat after dark. I have watched trucks and certain "suspect" small barges that came in and followed my bootlegger friends around when I thought I was most inconvenient for them.[45]*

Premm, with the insouciance of youth, not only considered the job a lark but also bragged that she had been shot at several times. She added that one bootlegger, mistaking another woman for her, pushed the woman off the docks into shallow water. It turned out that the other woman was another bootlegger's wife.[46]

———❧———

31

Is HUNTINGTON HARBOR OR Cold Spring Harbor being used for rumrunning? That was the question being asked by the *Long Islander* newspaper in September 1923. Local rumor claimed that a mysterious boat was spotted flashing a light in the middle of the night. Officials received an anonymous note that Eagle Dock in Cold Spring Harbor was going to be used to unload a cargo of rum. Jack Trainer, the local traffic officer, along with a party of special deputies, set up watch. Trainer and his cohort were disappointed that night, as the rumor was false.[47]

THE *DRAGON*, A BLACK-HULLED former submarine chaser, quietly moored in Port Jefferson Harbor for several weeks in the late fall of 1923. Just a short distance from the public dock, the crew kept to themselves and would occasionally fly the Canadian flag. One day, the ship vanished for two days before returning to its mooring. Locals noticed that the ship was riding low in the water. As the days gradually passed, the ship slowly rose up higher and higher as if some unseen weight was being slowly removed. Speculation abounded in the village over the ship.

The customs patrol boat *Mirage* spotted the *Dragon* on the move during its most recent trip and followed the vessel back to anchorage. When officials boarded the ship, they found the six men aboard were not from Canada but Manhattan and Brooklyn. Also aboard the ship was a large cache of liquor secreted below decks. The newspaper speculated that another incident may

Since 1797, Port Jefferson's harbor has had shipbuilding yards. The busy harbor allowed the ship *Dragon* to blend in for several weeks. *Author's collection.*

have been connected with the *Dragon*: three gunmen were in a wreck when the Long Island Rail Road train collided with their car in St. James. They may have been on their way to meet the *Dragon* and escort the cargo back to the city.[48]

SOME OF THE ILLEGAL cargos of booze were apprehended by authorities, and some were apprehended by local residents. In Sayville, one warm December night, a rumrunning truck became mired in the mud along the side of the road. When the driver left the truck to get help, the abandoned truck was soon raided by local men, who carried off the entire load.[49]

FIRST BUILT IN 1906 for Emory L. Ford Jr., the yacht *Thelma Phoebe* started out as the steam yacht *Galatea*. At 140 feet long, the 157-ton ship was made of steel was considered luxurious in 1907. The ship was sold around 1915 to creosote industrialist Sylvester W. Labrot Sr. before becoming a navy ship during World War 1. Rechristened the USS *Onward*, the ship patrolled the U.S. coastline. In 1921, the ship was excessed and sold to Roland T. Symonette of Nassau, Bahamas. On April 29, 1923, the rechristened *Thelma Phoebe* was approximately fifteen miles off Montauk in the grip of a violent storm. The storm's strong winds had ripped the rudder off the vessel, leaving it adrift.

> *By 7 a.m., the crew, straining to maintain their stations in the storm, caught a glimpse of land dead ahead through fog and rain, but could nothing to alter course.…Slowly the* Thelma Phoebe *drifted towards the rocks, pitching heavily in the seas which swept the yacht from stem to stern.…She grounded, all the while withstanding the impact of the mountainous waves now breaking over the decks.*[50]

The ship wrecked on the shores of Fishers Island. The only casualty of the wreck was the yacht's cook, Isaac Johnson, who panicked and jumped overboard, becoming tangled in the long strands of a nearby seaweed bed and drowned.

The Fishers Island Coast Guard Station found wreckage coming ashore the next morning and began combing the shoreline for the ship. "The Coast

One of the many ships that wrecked on the shores of Fishers Island. Although the crew members were arrested, they were eventually released. *Courtesy of the Henry L. Ferguson Museum Collection.*

The Coast Guard standing guard over some of the cargo from the *Thelma Phoebe. Courtesy of the Henry L. Ferguson Museum Collection.*

U.S. COAST GUARD STATION, FISHERS ISLAND, N.Y.

Fishers Island was seldom the planned destination of rumrunners; however, due to mishap and storms, boats occasionally crashed on the beaches of the island. *Author's collection.*

Guard log book entry reports; "Boat was very close to shore and crew were found in a small thicket drinking whiskey. The master of the vessel Harold Johnson reported his…cook as missing. He, with six seamen were taken into custody and sent to station under guard."[51] The station soon had to call in additional men to help gather up the whiskey, which was scattered all over the shore. Word of the wreck quickly spread, and soon two hundred of the island's five hundred residents, plus many of the soldiers from nearby Fort H.G. Wright, were scavenging the *Thelma Phoebe*'s cargo as quickly as it washed up on shore. So many of the soldiers from the fort became intoxicated on their illicit finds that the guardhouse was full and the officers were unable to muster enough men for regular guard detail that night. At one point, a small group of soldiers confronted the Coast Guard men guarding the wreck seeking to board the vessel and search for more booze. It took a Coast Guard officer drawing his weapon to make the group back off. The vessel was reported to have been carrying 2,400 cases of scotch, of which only 864 cases made it into authorities' hands.

After an investigation by customs officials, the captain and crew were released, based on a technicality: the yacht's paperwork stated that its destination was Halifax, Canada, and not the United States, so officials couldn't bring the men up on charges of breaking the Volstead Act.[52]

1924

Bringing liquor to the shores of the East End was no easy task, a rumrunner facing the local Coast Guard soon learned. Rumrunners bringing the booze ashore from the rum line tried an assortment of tactics to elude the Coast Guard—everything from disguising their cargo to trying to outrun their opponents. Local fisherman were often not opposed to making a fast buck by bringing a couple of bottles back mixed in with their haul.

In 1924, the sloop *Elizabeth Wilson* of Greenport was seized and brought to New London by the Coast Guard destroyer *Jouett*. During a routine check off Block Island, the sloop was searched, and officials found the vessel had a small quantity of whiskey mixed in with its cargo of codfish.[53]

To cope with the uptick in rumrunning activity on the East End, the federal government decided to establish a floating base in Greenport Harbor. As the *County Review* newspaper account observed:

> *It would appear that the government is planning to exert every effort to up a stop to rum-running on eastern Long Island but it is a fact that an abundance of liquor is being brought ashore from the ships anchored outside the twelve mile limit and the rum running boats are having little difficulty in eluding the patrols. It is reported that prominent business men on eastern Long Island have made fortunes during the past year financing the boats engaged in rum running.*[54]

Moored on the left, the Coast Guard ship *Joulett* was one of a fleet cruising the waters around Long Island searching for rumrunners. *Courtesy of the U.S. Coast Guard.*

Early during Prohibition, the Coast Guard had a station in Greenport Harbor to patrol eastern Long Island. Later, the station was moved to New London. *Author's collection.*

ACCORDING TO THE *COUNTY Review*, Suffolk County had 2,045 cases of liquor seized by officials in March. The alcohol was valued at $60,695, at a time when a pound of coffee cost $0.35. In just a couple of days, officials in Patchogue caught a Nash touring car with 16 cases of scotch; two days later in Smithtown, Harold Larm and L.M. King, both of Southampton, were apprehended in an REO truck with 60 cases of whiskey. That evening in Center Moriches, a Buick roadster with 16 cases of scotch being driven by W.C. Thiele of Southampton and a Studebaker touring car with 17 cases of champagne being driven by W.M. Schaffer of Sag Harbor and Henry Theile of Water Mill were nabbed. In each case, authorities acquired not only the contraband liquor but also the vehicles, which were later sold at auction.[55]

Made for hauling heavy loads, the REO Speedwagon trucks were made by the REO Motor Car Company, named after its owner, Ransom Eli Olds. *From the* County Review, *August 6, 1925, page 20.*

Distressed by reports of the amount of liquor being smuggled into the country across Long Island, Reverend Dr. G.M. Brown of the Patchogue Methodist Church exclaimed to the *County Review*, "Long Island, which is also termed Liquor Island…happens to be the wettest spot in the entire country."[56]

JANUARY SAW A TERRIBLE tragedy at Fire Island Inlet when nine men drowned. It all started when William D. Eccleston, formerly of Orient but more recently of Bay Shore, bought a launch. Eccleston, known across Long Island as a manager of "moving picture theaters," had gone to Rockaway midweek with John "Virginia" Groen, a summer resident of Bay Shore, and James Williams of Hicksville to pick up his new motorboat *Electra*. The group left Rockaway at lunch and headed toward Fire Island. Suddenly, the weather changed: the wind began to pick up, and the water became turbulent. Tossed around like a cork, the men on the *Electra* had no choice but to brave the storm and attempt to get through the now hazardous Fire Island Inlet. The storm soon drove the boat onto a sandbar, and the trio spent the night bailing water and fighting the storm.

When Eccleston failed to return home that night, his wife panicked and began searching for someone to go out in the storm to search for him. It wasn't until the next morning that a pilot with a hydroplane took off from Babylon and spotted the men in the stranded boat.

By the afternoon, a rescue party made up of nine men and the pilot set out with Captain Arnold Mayne in the motorboat *Sid*. The water was still turbulent, but the rescue crew forged ahead, soon spotting the *Electra*, which was coming apart from the beating of the waves. The *Sid* managed to get close enough to pull the three men, shaking from exposure from their long ordeal, aboard and started back.

The men on the *Sid* soon discovered that the wind, instead of dying down, had grown stronger, and the seas were rising. A wave smashed the rudder, and unable to navigate, the boat was helpless in the storm. The waves breaking over the boat swept nine of the men overboard, leaving only Eccleston, Gerald Donaldson, William McDonald and James Delaney onboard. The Coast Guard, aware of the rescue mission, had also tried to launch their boats, but the storm beat them back.

At Oak Island Off Babylon, L. I.

Near the Robert Moses Causeway, Oak Island sits just east of Captree and the entrance into the Great South Bay. *Courtesy of the Oysterponds Historical Society, Orient, New York.*

Joe Murdock launched his thirty-foot powerboat with two other men and headed out to the now floundering *Sid* and rescued the four remaining men on the *Sid*. Rumors soon started that the real reason the *Electra* was out in the foul weather was because Eccleston and his companions were trying to land a load of liquor.

On the heels of the storm, a severe cold snap froze the bay, and the bodies of the missing men were frozen under the ice. Searchers began to find the missing men's bodies as the ice began to break up. Charles "Ike" Cleaves of Babylon, Charles J. Boylan and Elbert A. Tillotson of Ithaca were the first to be found. John "Virginia" Groen and George Brandorf of Freeport were next. Arnold Main of Montgomery, Alabama; James Veltman and Arthur Noland of Babylon; and John Williams of Hicksville were eventually found. But the tragedy caused Chester O. Ketcham, president of the Village of Babylon, grief when he ordered flags in the village to be flown at half-staff in memory of the lost. Conflicting sentiments about rumrunning rose among residents, and a Civic Association meeting was scheduled to work the matter out. There was no news on the results of the meeting.[57]

When authorities began pulling over and searching trucks on a regular basis, bootleggers turned to large touring cars to transport their haul up the island. *From the* Patchogue Advance, *December 14, 1921, page 21.*

IN MARCH 1924, PETE Wells was out for a drive in his Packard automobile. As he drove through Eastport, he was one of several men stopped and searched by officials. Wells's car was found to have twenty-nine cases of liquor. Another man had another thirty cases, and a third car was found to have a mixture of sixty cases of booze covered with loaves of bread. In an effort to hide the crates, the bread had been stacked so the loaves could be seen through the windows. Apparently, this was not the first time the bread had been used as a disguise. Officers found the loaves to be very stale during their search of the vehicle.[58]

FEDERAL OFFICERS HAD A problem: liquor was flowing like a river from east of the Shinnecock Canal to New York City. In an effort to stem the tide, M.J.C. Phillips, C.E. Schroeder and C.D. Coombs were assigned to clean up the area. The officials caught Daniel McInerney of Brooklyn and William Lewis of Patchogue in a truck with seventy cases of scotch as they passed through Southampton. Another truck filled with cabbages was stopped and unloaded by officials, who found the center of the cargo was over one hundred cases of Irish and scotch whiskey.[59]

WHAT IS A REASONABLE rate for renting a motorboat? This was the question that was laid before the Supreme Court in Riverhead by William D. Eccleston and Harold Mulford of Bay Shore. Both men agreed that some boat owners on the Great South Bay had made even more than $250 a day in renting out their motorboats. Eccleston was suing August Schneff of Baldwin to be reimbursed for the loss of four days of rent on his motorboat. The boat, which was reputed to be one of the fastest in the area, had been purchased from Schneff by Eccleston, who then rented the boat to Mulford. After a couple of days, Schneff, apparently wanted the boat back, pulled out the carburetor and wiring, effectively stranding the boat. Judge Stephen Callaghan must have smelled a rat, because his question was to Mulford: what was he doing with a boat that cost $250 a day? "Why piloting other boats through the Fire Island Inlet," virtuously replied Mulford. The judge then turned to Eccleston and asked if the cargos were wet or dry. Eccleston was awarded only $150 to replace his carburetor.[60]

AS THE NET TO capture bootleggers tightened, the methods of smuggling the contraband liquor across Long Island became increasingly elaborate. Prohibition agents Smith and Phelps got a tip that a cargo of booze had been landed two weeks earlier and was going to be moved soon. The haul was packed into seven cars and moved as far west as Eastport when word came down that officers had been alerted and were searching for the cars. The lead driver quickly turned back to Sag Harbor and hid his prize. Stymied in their search for the elusive load of liquor, Smith and Phelps spent some time idly studying a green Ajax Motor Oil truck. The men had heard a story that the tanker had been used recently to slip a load of booze

Although seldom used (or at least not caught), oil trucks would have had plenty of room to transport cases of liquor. *Library of Congress.*

into the city. Searching for an alternative mode of transportation, the lead driver of the illicit cargo also spotted a green tanker truck emblazoned with "Ajax Motor Oil." Thinking to disguise the truck as a legitimate business that worked across all of Long Island, he purloined the tanker and painted the truck red with "Havoline Crude Oil" on the side. He reloaded his cargo in the tanker and set out. About a mile east of Lake Grove on Middle Island Road, the truck was pulled over by the officers, who told the driver that they needed some gas. He offered them half of the can of gas he had in the cab and offered to pour it into their tank. There he observed to the officers that their tank was half full and didn't need the gas. The agents quickly demurred—perhaps their car's feed pipe had been stopped up—as they noticed that green paint was showing through under the red paint of the tanker. Suspicious of the tanker but unable to figure out if it was carrying any crates of alcohol, the officers reluctantly let the truck and driver on its way. As the truck pulled away, the officers compared observations, and one noticed that the driver had red paint on his overalls.

Realizing that the driver had repainted the truck to hide it, the officers leaped in their car to chase down the truck. This time, they arrested the driver, and when they unbolted the covers on the tanker they discovered it filled with 125 cases of liquor.[61]

AS THE BATTLE BETWEEN the Coast Guard and the rumrunners continued, the use of deadly force also intensified between the two groups. The crew of the new patrol boat *Shark* reported that three attempts were made to ram them in August 1924. One of the men was thrown overboard during an attack but was rescued. In retaliation, the *Shark* opened fire with its Lewis machine gun and unloaded six hundred shots into the ship *William 18*. The motorboat was carrying one thousand cases of scotch worth $40,000. Baldwin M. Raymond of Norfolk, William Herlacher of Manhattan and Alfred Reiter of Greenport were placed under arrest.[62]

That same week, a powerboat, *K13524*, was seized by the Coast Guard with one hundred sacks of whiskey near Fire Island Inlet. Fred Foster and Lawrence Baldwin of Bay Shore along with Edward Bowen of Northport and William D. Eccleston of Hicksville were captured.[63]

Situated roughly at the halfway point on Long Island, Bay Shore was one of largest "streams" from which liquor flowed into New York City. *Author's collection.*

———— ∞ ————

PROHIBITION AGENTS PHELPS AND Gosnell's attention was caught in early May by a speeding truck whizzing past them on its way from Sag Harbor to Quogue. Following the truck and demanding it pull over, only to be ignored, the agents soon crowded the truck and forced it to a halt off the road. Frank Wilson, the driver, claimed that the truck was loaded with soft drinks, but they could look it over. The officers then started to unload the truck, and under the upper layers of soda were twenty cases of whiskey.[64]

———— ∞ ————

THE LURE OF MAKING a lot of money quickly coaxed the brave into trying their hand at rumrunning. Rumor had it in Montauk that a man got a contract to move six thousand cases from Rum Row to shore. He charged $7 a case, which was up from the $2 a case that was being charged locally before the revenue officers and Coast Guard began enforcing the law in the area. The contractor's expenses for the venture included renting a large fishing boat for $2,000 for three months. His profit was $40,000 for six weeks of work, a fortune at a time when a shopper could get 14 oranges for $0.25.[65]

———— ∞ ————

OFF ORIENT POINT, THE motorboats *Sadie E. Nickerson* and the *Theodore*, each carrying five hundred cases of whiskey, were seized by the Coast Guard. The crew of the two ships—from Connecticut, New York City and one man from New Orleans—admitted that they hatched their smuggling plans at the Seamen's Institute in Manhattan.[66]

———— ∞ ————

L.W. ROTHSTEIN OF SOUTHAMPTON was not having a good day. He had loaded his roadster with as much booze as it could hold and was moving his haul as quickly as he could up to the city. On Jericho Turnpike in Huntington, Rothstein suddenly lost control of his car, which veered off the road and flipped three times before coming to rest on its side in the woods. A witness to the accident quickly reported it to the local constable. When the constable arrived, the driver had disappeared, leaving behind 312 bottles of liquor. The sheriff traced the owner of the vehicle from the license plate, and several hours later, Rothstein, surprisingly uninjured, was found and arrested. Rothstein later confessed that he had been drinking while driving, thus causing his own problems.[67]

> *It is reported that liquor has been smuggled ashore at Amagansett bathing station and at Egypt beach, this village, recently. The rum runners evidently feel safer sometimes to land their cargos on the south side than to run through the sound and bays.*[68]

ONE OF THE PROBLEMS of enforcing Prohibition was the revolving door of justice. The rumrunners and bootleggers had the money and the ability to easily make bail and walk away from the charges against them. Five men in Smithtown who were caught by a squad of state troopers with twenty-nine cases of liquor on a Monday night in 1924 were out by Friday. One of the smugglers, Louis Scala, had tried to pull a pistol on the troopers. However, the hammer of the gun had snagged on his pocket and he was quickly disarmed before being arrested. His cohorts, John Porkey, Phillip Napolitano, Vincent Varone and Albert Scabella, were also subdued and arraigned on charges of violating the Volstead Act. The group had been caught because their high-powered car was spotted speeding through the village toward Smithtown's Long Beach. Constable William Howell and Motorcycle Patrolman Joseph Jirik began knocking on doors in the area before receiving a tip that the liquor was being stored in one of the houses. The liquor was reputed to be part of one thousand cases that had been unloaded from a German ship. After calling for assistance from the troopers, the officials approached the house in question. In front of the building was a sand pile with five men sitting on it. Nearby were three cases of liquor. The search of the house revealed the other twenty-six cases. It was believed that the captured cases were the last of the haul that was landed on the beach earlier in the evening.[69]

IN THE SPRING OF 1924, the violence in the struggle between officials and smugglers moved up several notches. A half mile from Eastport on Manorville Road, a disagreement leading to a shootout occurred between two opposing factions in the Ku Klux Klan. Special Constable Ferdinand

Downs of East Quogue was prominent in the Klan. A week earlier, he had been removed from his job as Southampton town traffic officer. Residents had been complaining that Downs was stopping motorists without justification in his quest to catch bootleggers. When Downs pulled over Eleanor Corrigan just over the border in Brookhaven Town, he had gone too far.[70] However, Officer Downs was not without supporters. At the next Southampton Board Meeting, Downs's supporters besieged the town board and demanded he be rehired.

Working as a traffic officer was what paid the bills. Downs's evenings were spent working at his passion. Along with like-minded members of his local Klan, Downs collaborated with Prohibition agents to track and capture bootleggers passing through the area.

On Friday night, May 16, Ferdinand J. Downs was at Eastport, around 10:45 p.m. He was, as usual, scouting for bootleggers. In the company of Joseph and Raymond Payne of Quogue, Walter Gordon of Eastport and Carlos Wilcox of Speonk, Downs and his companions crammed themselves into a car that had been rented by Prohibition agents. Downs wore clothes that were very similar to his regular uniform. Cruising the roads, the men soon saw a 1924 Buick seven-passenger sedan whiz past them going the opposite way on Montauk Highway in Quogue. Downs excitedly exclaimed he saw cases of whiskey piled in the car.

After a four-mile chase, the vigilantes managed to pass the Buick at Westhampton and pulled over to prepare to stop the other car. However, the rumrunner saw their trap, turned off his headlights, performed a U-turn and headed back east to a byway.

Soon realizing that the other car was trying to go around them using another road, Down and his companions raced their vehicle to the crossroad in Eastport where the Buick would emerge. Again, the rumrunner spotted their car, switched off his headlights and turned around and backtracked toward Manorville.

Local newspapers seldom had headlines that stretched across the entire page. But the murder of Downs was sensational enough to merit the front page. *From the* County Review, *October 24, 1924, page 1.*

As the men began chasing the Buick in earnest, shots rang out. Downs returned fire and grabbed a flashlight to try to get a light on the fleeing car's license plate. A bullet quickly knocked the flashlight out of Downs's hand. Soon a rain of bullets began hitting the pursuer's vehicle. Downs, who had climbed out onto the running board toward the front of the car, was struck in the back of the head and killed instantly.

Downs's companions continued to return fire until they ran out of ammunition, and then they left off the high-speed pursuit. Realizing the seriousness of Downs's injury, they rushed him to the nearest doctor's office, where he was declared dead on arrival.

A reported five thousand people attended the funeral. His killer, Patrick Ryan, a former New York City police officer, was indicted in court as the funeral took place. "Clergymen in the regalia of the Klan, standing at the open grave in the flickering shadows of a blazing cross, hailed Downs as a martyr to the 'pampered bootleggers,' asserted that he had died because he had spurned bribes and done his duty."[71]

SURPRISINGLY, THE MOST TIP-OFFS about potential bootlegging trips came from one specific group, the Ku Klux Klan. The membership went out of its way to assist Prohibition agents. They not only passed along tips, either by telephone or in person, but they also lent agents their automobiles, allowing them to hide in plain sight. Klan members switched license plates and even volunteered their wives and children to ride as passengers. Phone tips to agents many times included the informant continuing to follow the suspect until agents could catch up and pull the vehicle over.[72]

The federal government needed more bodies to combat the smugglers, reported the *Long Islander*, and set up a new protective system. Firemen in several towns were now required to answer the call for assistance. The firemen were instructed to tumble "out of bed, grabbing shotguns, rifles, revolvers or anything they could get their hands on, and rush to the location assigned." In Commack, the department had to place large trucks across the roadways to stop all traffic in either direction, while in other areas main thoroughfares were also blocked.[73]

In November 1924, the *East Hampton Star* noted what it called the first real attempt made to stop the flow of liquor coming into Long Island. A river of alcohol was being shipped from Montauk Point up to New York City by way of an assortment of vehicles traveling over the local roads. For locals, the smuggling was a somewhat open secret; for R.Q. Merrick, the chief Prohibition agent for New York and northern New Jersey, it was just one of many ongoing sources of frustration. His newest strategy to turn the river into a trickle had him sending agents out to block the cinder road in Napeague Beach. There the agents stopped and searched every suspicious vehicle that passed. Agents seized eleven automobiles and arrested thirteen men. The local newspaper noted that the seized cars were parked up and down the side of the road during the operation.

According to a statement made by Merrick, "The number of seizures and arrests made last week exceeded the average for any month since the inauguration of the Coast Guard Patrol....We have not averaged more than two or three truck seizures a week." Merrick's own agents speculated that the rumrunners had a new strategy, waiting until the agents were tied up in Brooklyn Federal Court testifying to openly race their cargos up the island. Agents Zegel and Gosnell confided to the *East Hampton Star* that they suspected that runners were so organized that even the telephone operators were on the smugglers' payroll because phone tips seldom paid off.[74]

Howard Seaman, his son, George Sears and Chris Olsen decided to move their cargo of liquor in broad daylight at Seaman's dock in Montauk. As the men were loading up their touring cars with three hundred cases of scotch and champagne, Peter J. Sullivan, chief of the U.S. Customs Marine Patrol, and several of his men came for an unannounced inspection of the area. The rumrunners were caught red-handed. The liquor came from one of the thirteen ships in the rum fleet lying at anchor just outside the U.S. territorial waters.[75]

The revenue men in Montauk made another easy seizure in May 1924 when the fishing boat they were chasing beached itself. The owner of the boat, realizing that the agents were closing in, quickly slipped over the side of the boat and disappeared inland. On the abandoned ship was thirty-six cases of liquor.[76]

In Montauk, the Coast Guard appeared to be tripping over rumrunners, F.D. Warner, the captain of the Hither Plain Coast Guard Station, surprised

A bird's-eye view of the Montauk shoreline and the warehouses used by the fishing fleets lining the coast by Fort Pond. *Courtesy of the Southold Historical Museum, Southold, New York.*

Oliver Beckwith, the son of a local fisherman, with 115 cases of liquor as he was landing his haul from a dory onto the beach. However, a powerboat with another 150 cases trailing the dory escaped into the night. The *East Hampton Star* speculated that Beckwith was probably moving the cases to a storehouse and was seeking to sell the load gradually to prospective buyers. It also acknowledged that "fish dealers in Montauk are complaining of the shortage of fish and lobsters and it is believed that the rumrunning is one of the main causes." The boatmen of the area were making five dollars a case for transporting liquor ashore, an attractive change of pace from the uncertainty of fishing.[77]

⸺✺⸺

A RUMOR REACHED THE ears of Sheriff Amza Briggs that a big haul was going to be brought ashore in Montauk in February 1924. Quickly, he summoned his deputy officers and set out for Montauk. The group paused in East Hampton to pick up two local officers, and the group continued on to Montauk. During the trip, they passed several speeding trucks, fully loaded and heading west, and saw several of the bootleggers' spotters.

When the group made it to Amagansett, they pulled into the railroad station, turned off their headlights and waited. The local spotter for the smugglers cruised slowly by on the Montauk Highway. Soon, another car, with a box tied to its rear, pulled into the station, passed the officers and, apparently not spotting them, turned around and roared back the way it had come.

The two cars with Briggs and his men started up and trailed behind the fleeing car. Just before reaching Montauk, another car powered past them intent on warning the bootleggers of their presence. The officers went straight to Frank Parson's dock, where they discovered what was called the largest smuggling operation seen to date. Fifteen trucks, both light and heavy-duty, were being loaded up, as were a number of touring and closed cars lining the road waiting their turn to load.

As their cars glided to a stop, the magnitude of the operation sank into the officer's minds. Some twenty men from the nearby fishing shacks silently appeared unfazed by the agents' appearance. The men watched unworried as the officers climbed out of their cars. There was not a box of liquor anywhere in sight.

The deputies then heard from the dock the sound of wood cases being unloaded. Fully armed, Briggs and his men quickly moved to investigate. Barely tied to the dock by one rope was a 110-foot, black-hulled speedboat piled with liquor. Next to the boat on the dock was a flat transport cart loaded with at least fifty cases ready to be moved up the dock to the waiting trucks.

The officials instantly moved to take charge of the situation and ordered everyone to freeze. While some of the officers secured the smugglers on the dock and took charge of the alcohol, the rest of the group moved toward the boat. As the first official reached the deck of the speedboat, one of the crew released the mooring line, and the boat, under the control of the current, swung away from the dock. Quickly realizing his peril of one officer against a crew of twelve rumrunners, the officer leaped toward shore as the ship moved away. While the officials had the men at Parson's dock quelled, they could clearly hear other powerboats being unloaded into trucks at other nearby docks.

Biggs must have been beside himself with impotent rage and self-recrimination for not bringing along more men on his raiding party. Instead of being able to boast of capturing a huge haul, he was only able to seize the sixty cases that were on the dock.

One of the deputies asked the truck drivers why they were not loading and found out that the operation had been tipped off to their presence by

On the far eastern end, Montauk has had a bustling shoreline, used by local fisherman from all over the east end of Long Island. *Courtesy of the Southold Historical Museum, Southold, New York.*

a spotter who had seen them on the road between the Shinnecock Canal and Southampton.

The officers and the smugglers were at an impasse. The officers did not have enough manpower to get control of the entire situation and arrest all of those involved in the scheme. The bootleggers did not want to give up their cargo and very much wanted to avoid a gun battle with the sheriff's deputies. In the end, an unspoken gentleman's agreement seemed to prevail. Briggs and his men captured the sixty cases of liquor that were untouched on the dock. Since no one present was willing to admit to being privy to the contents of the cases, no one was arrested.

However, the night had one more event for Briggs and his deputies after they loaded up one of the trucks with their booty. A deputy hopped into the driver's seat and began driving the truck with its captured load to Riverhead. As the truck passed through Amagansett, it broke down and probably put the icing on Briggs's night. He ended up having go wake up a nearby resident Frank Conklin to borrow a truck and have his men transfer the load to get it to Riverhead.[78]

EARLY ON A SATURDAY morning, Special Enforcement Agent Merchant Phelps was passing through Great River when he spotted a big moving van being followed by a car. The side of the van was emblazed with the name John G. Carlson of Bay Ridge. As he pulled the van over, the car—with what seemed to be the owner of the load—also pulled over.

Agent Phelps had the driver and his assistant open up the back of the truck to reveal a load of bedding, furniture and the overwhelming stench of booze. Mixed in with the household goods were 250 cases of champagne, gin, brandy and scotch. As soon as the driver of the car learned that the truck and its cargo was being confiscated, he became extremely upset and began exhibiting symptoms of a possible heart attack, alarming all of the others, who feared he was dying. Phelps somehow managed to get the ill man medical attention and take into custody the moving truck driver and his assistant as well as secure the contents of the truck.[79]

───❊───

The thinking that bad storms were the bootlegger's friend was foremost on the mind of Special Prohibition Enforcement Agents Merchant Phelps and Lowell Smith. So when a snowy and sleeting nor'easter blew through Long Island in March 1924, the pair were out patrolling the roads. In Eastport, the agents spotted four men driving two trucks. Wanting to stop the vehicles but not expecting them to willingly pull over, the two agents raced in front of the trucks, stepped out of their car onto Montauk Highway and drew their revolvers, giving the truck drivers no alternative but to stop. Phelps and Smith's instincts to stop the trucks proved to be on target. Both trucks were filled with a cargo of 150 cases of various types of liquor. Half an hour later, the pair pulled over a large truck. As the truck pulled over to the shoulder of the road, the car that was following it made a speedy U-turn and raced back the way it came.

The agents quickly summoned the local constable to take charge of the driver and truck. Then they began following the tracks that the car left in the snow. The car's tracks were soon joined by two trucks that also turned around. The weather was not favoring the bootleggers. One of the trucks skidded off the road and became mired in the mud. The other truck, needing gas, was caught where it stopped at a corner filling station. All three trucks hailed from Greenport and were heading up to New York City. The combined cargo of the three trucks was about one thousand crates.

RUMRUNNING IN SUFFOLK COUNTY

When one of the prisoners attempted to escape, the agents called the local Ku Klux Klan for reinforcements. Nine Klan members quickly joined the agents and helped escort the prisoners and the trucks up to the city. One of the truck drivers bragged that the officers missed two other trucks. Phelps quickly sent a message to Sheriff Biggs to be on the lookout for the missing trucks. Both were found marooned six miles west of Riverhead. As soon as one driver saw the sheriff's officers approaching, he bolted toward the woods and escaped. The other driver, Herman Schwebes of Middle Island, was not as fast on his feet and was quickly caught and placed under arrest. One of the trucks was disguised with the logo Sunrise Transportation, the other proclaimed it as Stone's Van of New York. Both vehicles became stuck in the muddy road that extended from the end of the paved roadway. The agents believed that most of the load came onshore in Greenport and was traveling directly to New York City.[80]

ONE MONDAY MORNING IN April, Prohibition officials were busy across Long Island. In Smithtown, at 9:30 a.m., officers pulled over a truck loaded with piano boxes. On closer inspection inside the boxes, each was filled with booze.[81]

IN AMAGANSETT, A MAN was captured by officers. As they were transporting him up to Riverhead for booking, the prisoner realized that the car was going to pass his house in Water Mill. The man leaned forward to the officers and asked urgently if they could stop at his house so he could telephone his wife and let her know what had happened. Surprisingly, the officers agreed and stopped at their prisoner's home. Inside, the man called his wife and asked her "to telephone his brother that he was 'pinched'" and to come down and furnish bail. She replied, 'All right, but B—— just phoned that he was pinched and wants you to bail him [out]."[82]

TWO MEN DRIVING A car westward were stopped by officials in Moriches. As the agents approached the car, one of the men flicked something out of the window that landed nearby on the road. Turns out the car was loaded with alcohol, and the item that was thrown out the window was a badge that belonged to one of the men in the car—a deputy sheriff from Nassau County.[83]

—————⊗⊗⊗⊗—————

IN NOVEMBER 1924, THE *Brooklyn Daily Eagle* made a survey of the rumrunning and bootlegging activity across Long Island and declared that the business was growing by leaps and bounds all along the shoreline of the island. The article noted that a barrel of scotch on the ships ranged from $13 to $22, but the bootleggers' cost to his customers started at $40.[84]

The business of liquor smuggling had become not only big business on Long Island, but also very organized. Newspapers claimed that the hub of the business was centered in Massapequa and that some of the biggest streams of booze were flowing through Amityville, Bay Shore, Babylon and Freeport. In some places, bootleggers and customers knew that different brands of liquor were stored in different places and where they had to visit to get their favorite brands.[85]

"'Damn those rumrunners,' remarked a Long Island game warden.... 'They were so thick in Jones Inlet yesterday afternoon that I couldn't navigate my boat. Then the flag went up and they all started full speed out to sea. They nearly ran me down.'" When the flag that signaled that the Coast Guard was occupied elsewhere went up on shore, a veritable platoon of speedboats left their hidden alcoves along the shoreline to make the round trip to Rum Row.

Since the Coast Guard selected boats that were riding low in the water, rumrunners had started throwing away the packing crates and packing the bottles into bags to lighten the loads they packed on board. They also started attaching a buoy onto the bags for later retrieval in case they needed to dump the load overboard.[86]

The bulk of the business was also starting to shift up the island and from the south shore to the north shore as federal agents made the bootlegging more difficult. While the majority of the rumrunners along the East End and south shore were locals, the new rumrunners starting to crowd the high bluffs of the north shore were from the city or farther afield.[87]

—————⊗⊗⊗⊗—————

Edwin Burnett on Flying Point Road in Water Mill was checking his fishing nets along Mecox Beach when he saw a two-masted schooner come to rest nearby. Two small boats were lowered into the water with fifteen men who rowed ashore. When the men reached the beach, they abandoned the boats in the water and asked him for directions to Sag Harbor. The schooner, like the two small boats, was abandoned and left to drift away on the current. Locals speculated that ship was a rumrunner that had finished selling its cargo, and the men Burnett spoke to were the crew heading for home or their next job.[88]

On a cold November evening, about one thousand feet from the Fire Island Coast Guard Station, an empty powerboat, rocking in the waves, drifted ashore. On board the boat were twenty cases of whiskey. Other crates of liquor, apparently from the boat, bobbed in the water nearby. Local fishermen observing the situation reported that although officials had spotted the boat, none of the guardsmen approached the vessel or the drifting crates.

The following day, a group of men from the mainland arrived and towed the boat out past the breaking waves and toward the mainland. They paid no attention to the loose crates of booze still floating in the waters around them. The fishermen, seeing the opportunity, quickly snagged and brought aboard the loose crates. It was thought that during its nighttime run the powerboat hit and stuck on one of the local sandbars. The crew, in an effort to refloat the boat, threw part of the cargo overboard. When that failed, the crew made their way to the Coast Guard station; the station crew brought them to the mainland, where they could get help.[89]

Agents Phelps, Gosnell, Smith, Schmeelk and Zegel, working the East End, saw an uptick in smuggling for the 1924 holiday season. Although they felt that the amount of liquor being transported to the far East End had slowed, they still caught seven cars loaded with booze between Amagansett and East Islip. Peter Pell and Richard Ranahan made it to East Islip with fifteen cases before being caught. Floyd Bill of Sag Harbor was picked up with thirty cases in Amagansett. Edward Neumeyer was stopped in his

Dodge coupe in Southampton with twenty cases of champagne. Amba Rattl of Woodside was caught in Eastport, his Pierce Arrow packed with thirty-eight cases of scotch. A Southampton man calling himself John Doe was found with twenty-five cases in his car. John Klein had thirty cases of whiskey in his Packard, and Pasquale Benicola was stopped in East Hampton with twenty cases of vermouth.[90]

———❦———

With so much booze coming into the area, even a new Prohibition officer, also known as a dry agent, could get lucky and stumble onto a rumrunner. At 3:00 a.m. on a humid August night in 1924, the *Pacific* shot into the Greenport docks hurriedly, made fast its lines and started unloading. New dry agent James Ziegal, on his first night at work, stepped from the cover of a fish market and, with a drawn revolver, single-handedly forced the crew to surrender their cargo, worth $45,000.[91]

1925

You did not have to be involved in the rumrunning business to get swept up in the violence, as some residents quickly found out. In April 1925, Lloyd Hamilton and Edward Coleman along with their girlfriends went up to Bailey's Beach in Mattituck on a date to enjoy the romance of the beach at night. Out by the breakwater 10:30 p.m., the two couples soon heard a boat that sounded like it was run aground. They shouted out, asking if the people on the boat needed help. When someone on the boat said yes, the couples went nearby to Peter Wyckoff's house to get a third man to help move the boat.

When they returned to the site where they thought the boat was, they called out again. Suddenly from the water came a hail of machine gun bullets that peppered the beach. The would-be rescuers quickly dropped to the ground and found shelter. Three men from the boat then came ashore with a dory and began shooting blindly around the area with revolvers. Luckily, no one was killed.

An investigation later discovered that the ship in distress was a Coast Guard patrol boat. The patrol boat had been ordered to Mattituck Creek to intercept a suspected rum-smuggling vessel. The crew claimed they fired on the three men and two women in self-defense because they believed they were being fired on. Hamilton, who returned to the scene the next morning to get his car, told a newspaper reporter that he was sure that he had spotted crates of liquor on the Coast Guard ship's deck.[92]

Located on Long Island Sound, Bailey's Beach is sited at the mouth of Mattituck Creek. *Author's collection.*

DANGER TO RESIDENTS CAME not only from the water but also on the roads. An unidentified but well-known young man from Riverhead and his companion from Mattituck were out for a drive along the North Road traveling from Southold westward to Mattituck. Suddenly, an unidentified car began to bear down on them aggressively.

Fearful of bandits, the man began driving faster and faster, until both cars were hurdling down the road at a high rate of speed. The car eventually passed him on the North Road at Mattituck and forced him to stop at the point of a revolver. In the unidentified car were Prohibition enforcement officers. When the officers learned who the man was, they apologized for pulling him over, stating they thought they were chasing a bootlegger.

The man, shaken, in his interview with the newspaper, "severely denounced the resumption of the 'reign of terror' which resulted in the loss of many thousands of dollars in business in Suffolk County the summer before because tourists feared being indiscriminately held up by prohibition enforcement agents and others."[93]

Originally berthed in Peconic Bay by Greenport, the Coast Guard later moved its center of operations to New London, Connecticut. *Courtesy of the United States Coast Guard Historian and Laurie Friel.*

THE MOTORBOAT *BARBARA* OF Philadelphia "ran ashore and stranded high on the rocks east of Chocomount on Barley Field Reef [Fishers Island]....She was carrying 243 cases of whiskey. The crew of three were arrested and sent to New London. The Coast Guard had to maintain a strong guard through the night to stop Fort Wright soldiers from storming the vessel."[94]

After a year of using the floating base in Greenport, the Coast Guard base moved to Nantucket. Their reasoning was that they felt that the rumrunning on the East End of Long Island was under control.[95]

IN THE OPENING DAYS of 1925, the *Arco Felice II* and a smaller unnamed schooner began frequenting Huntington Harbor, bringing in supplies for those who still had a thirst after the New Year's revels. A four-masted schooner, *Arco Felice II* was a rare sight in 1925 and attracted the attention of the local fisherman and duck hunters. The ship hailed from Naples and battled its way across heavy seas to landed three thousand cases of scotch and champagne onto the beach at Huntington Harbor. As night fell, the ships quickly unloaded their cargo into trucks with Manhattan department store logos, which were guarded by men with rifles.

In the early light of dawn, reports of the ship made it to the Coast Guard commander, William Munter, who immediately gave orders for the Coast Guard ship *Red Wing* to capture the *Arco Felice II*. The Italian ship offered no resistance when the Coast Guard arrived and soon was under tow up to

New York Harbor. Because of the large size of the ship, the *Arco Felice II* had to be anchored off of the Statue of Liberty. While the Coast Guard did a thorough search of the ship, only three cases of liquor were found. Under questioning, the captain of the ship admitted to having "thrown" overboard over eight thousand cases. The Coast Guard officials decided to also notify the Immigration Service about the ship possibly smuggling in illegal immigrants because several of the ship's crew had gone missing as well.[96]

A PIERCE-ARROW PULLED UP to a stop at a hotel in Smithtown. Hungry, the driver wandered inside for a bite to eat. Upon learning that one of the hotel guests, Patrick McIntrney, was going to catch the train to Brooklyn, he invited him to instead ride up to Brooklyn with him. The passenger probably soon began to wonder about his good fortune, as the driver began to accelerate, going faster and faster. Just west of Huntington, the Pierce-Arrow pulled out into opposing traffic to pass a slower-moving vehicle and smashed into Patsy Mastrianni, who was driving home to Huntington with his mother and nephew, Natal Leoni. The Pierce-Arrow overturned, and the front end tore off, while Mastrianni's car was ripped in two by the force of the impact.

Above: The remains of Patsy Mastrianni's car after a boot legger's car crashed into it. While the passengers in both cars were injured, no one died. *From the* Long Islander, *January 16, 1925, page 3.*

Right: A heavy-duty suspension and roomy passenger compartment made the Pierce-Arrow one of the favorite vehicles of bootleggers on Long Island. *From the* County Review, *September 17, 1925, page 10.*

Surprisingly, no one was killed. After a moment of shock, the driver of the Pierce-Arrow quickly recovered his wits, crawled out of the car and began running back toward Huntington. He soon flagged down two other Pierce-Arrows, both loaded with crates of booze, and crawled into one the vehicles, leaving his passenger still stunned in his wrecked car. People who stopped to help soon smelled the odor of scotch, which perfumed the air. Apparently wedged out of sight between the front and back seats was 20 cases of liquor, of which 125 bottles survived the accident. Officials later imparted that they believed that the ruined Pierce-Arrow and its driver were part of an eighteen-man liquor-hijacking crew that was operating in Huntington area.[97]

ONE NIGHT, A COLD Spring Harbor resident decided to spend the evening watching the rumrunners unloading their cargo down the beach from him on Eagle Dock. After a while, the resident thought of a way of maybe getting a bottle or two. He ambled down the beach to the dock and told one of the guards that "he knew what was going on and that he wanted a bottle or two to keep his mouth shut." But he didn't get a drink—instead, he got the muzzle of a gun pushed into his ribs and was told to sit down and rest. After the cargo was unloaded onto the vehicles that were going to carry it on the next leg of its trip, the men guarding the cargo each took a drink of whiskey from a small flask. After they had drained the contents, they handed the empty bottle to the resident and said, "Have a drink on me, Mr. Smarty," before driving off.[98]

THE RUMRUNNING MOTORBOAT *CECILE* of Sag Harbor and its crew of three Greek men, one of whom lived in Greenport, had been missing since August. The *Cecile*, powered with five-hundred-horsepower engines, was one of the fastest boats in the area and went out to Rum Row to pick up a load of liquor. The boat reached Rum Row, made a deal with a schooner and loaded up. It then seemingly disappeared from the face of the earth. A fire-charred hatch, believed to be from the *Cecile*, was found floating in the waters off Montauk Point. It was thought that the engines of the powerful boat backfired and set the boat on fire. Given up as lost, the boat was forgotten until it and its crew arrived in Capetown, South Africa, in November! No word was given on how the resourceful crew survived three months in a small open boat on the Atlantic Ocean.[99]

One of the most confusing cases of bootlegging and hijacking happened at the Benson Estate in 1925. Newspaper accounts of the events at the estate in Montauk each reported slightly different versions of what happened. Who was and wasn't present also changed depending on the newspaper.

In the 1880s, shipping millionaire Arthur Benson purchased most of Montauk Point to create a private hunting and vacation lodge for himself and select friends. In 1925, the property, known as the Benson Estate, was cared for by Frank Dickerson, who had a small hidden shack where he reputedly stored choice wines and liquors.

Jerry O'Keefe, Frank and Thomas Smith (whose real last name was Browski), William Shaber of Patchogue and William Delmadge (a new state trooper from St. James) had a scheme to get rich quick: the five men had found out that Dickerson was sitting on a fortune in liquor, and they were going to attempt to hijack the liquor stored on the Benson Estate.[100]

The men took a truck and possibly two cars and made their way from Patchogue out to Montauk. Meanwhile, Frank Dickerson and his assistant, Arthur Browngardt, were meeting with a group of men who were negotiating to purchase and move the liquor stash. The group had moved inside the house when Jerry O'Keefe began banging on the door.[101]

O'Keefe, pretending to be an official and wearing Delmadge's state trooper's badge, demanded that the group come out of the building and line up on the porch. As soon as the group emerged from the building, chaos ensued, and shots were fired. Delmadge was hit in the back, and Thomas Smith received a glancing shot in the head. The five hijackers' nerves quickly gave out, and they ran and jumped into one of their cars and attempted to escape. They had barely gotten to the roadway when they found themselves blocked by two cars. The hijackers were roughly pulled from their vehicle, and all except for the wounded Thomas Smith were forced to their knees.[102]

A man named Captain Eric Walker, who was believed to be a representative of a British liquor syndicate, demanded that Delmadge turn over his state trooper's hat, revolver and shield, remarking that he wanted them as souvenirs. Then he had his men, Lawrence P. Pleasants, Frederick W. Brown and George Steppits, all of Sag Harbor, beat up the hijackers. They were then loaded into an old Dodge car and told to go to the hospital. Instead, the group made their way to a nearby doctor to get patched up and then drove to Helen Smith's house in Patchogue to lie low.[103]

There the men began crafting different versions of the night's events. According to one of the Smith brothers, they received a telephone message from their father that someone had stolen their family truck. The brothers leaped into action, getting Shaber and Delmadge to pursue the truck to Montauk, where they discovered it in Dickerson's yard. The brothers claimed they were in the act of recovering their property when someone shot them.[104]

The other Smith brother claimed that they met O'Keefe and Delmadge while they were trying to pick up girls at the Port Jefferson train station. After remarking that it was a good night to transport a load of liquor up the city, his compatriots agreed and they all set off to Montauk.[105]

Delmadge stated to authorities that he was on short leave from the White Plains station and that he and the other three men went to the Dickerson shack and demanded that their two cars be filled with liquor or they would tell federal authorities about the stash. Delmadge said that there was a scuffle and he lost his badge and gun; then the door of the shack was slammed in their faces, and someone fired at them, severely wounding Thomas Smith and Delmadge. Delmadge, who was in uniform, after being patched up by the local doctor, was brought with his co-conspirators back to Patchogue to the Smith brothers' sister Helen's house to recuperate.[106]

According to Dickerson, he and his family were innocently asleep when the Smith brothers, Delmadge and Shaber arrived. Dickerson and his assistant Browngardt, who lived with the family, were awoken by the hijackers pounding on the front door. After being held in the front of his house for two hours, he heard someone shooting a gun and ran into the house. He also stated that about seventy cases of liquor had been taken from his hoard.[107]

The *Suffolk County News* said that the five hijackers arrived just as another man was trying to also make a deal for the liquor. When the four hijackers arrived, the man fled and came back with reinforcements. It was the reinforcements who beat up the hijackers and shot at them.[108]

Nine hours after the shooting, word of the attempted hijacking began making the rounds in

The People's Choice for
District Attorney

GEORGE W. HILDRETH

HE WILL SERVE YOU WELL

District Attorney George W. Hildreth was assistant district attorney in 1918 and became the district attorney in 1924. A job he held until 1929. *From the County Review, November 2, 1923, page 18.*

Montauk, and county authorities also heard the story. As soon as he heard the story, District Attorney Hildreth began to investigate. Lieutenant Lynch from the Bay Shore State Troopers Headquarters drove to Patchogue to bang on Helen Smith's door. When Lynch discovered Delmadge, riddled with buckshot holes, he hauled the man to his car.

Soon after, the Smith brothers and Shaber were arrested. Based on Delmadge's version of events, Lynch got a search warrant and went with backup to Dickerson's shack. There they found $200,000 worth of wine and liquor, as well as weapons, hidden in the building. Dickerson claimed that the liquor did not belong to him, but he was employed to guard it. Another thousand cases of whiskey were found hidden in the nearby swamps, bringing the total worth of the haul up to $250,000.

It was revealed at the trial that the group had been led by Jerry O'Keefe, a former state trooper. O'Keefe, who had fled the state when he learned of his compatriots' arrests, led the group while wearing Delmadge's badge. The hijackers not only demanded one hundred cases from Dickerson but also promised him "protection" if he complied with their demands.[109]

Confused? So were the newspaper articles and prosecutors. The hijackers were all indicted on burglary charges, because prosecutors were unable to get enough evidence to make bootlegging charges to stick. Everyone involved in

Built just before the Civil War, the Riverhead Courthouse is still being used. Behind it can be seen the local jail. *Author's collection.*

the fiasco, clammed up about moving the liquor. The case was revisited again a year later in an effort to close the case, which was left open, in the hope that O'Keefe and Eric Walker would eventually be caught. Delmadge was sentences to eight months in jail for bribery. Frank Dickerson was slapped with a $500 fine for possessing liquor. The other men were released on bail. The case against them was eventually dismissed.[110]

This was not the first time that the Smith brothers and their sister Helen had tangled with the law. Helen Smith, whom the newspapers dubbed the "Queen of Bootleggers of Long Island," was the owner of several cars. Her favorite was reputed to be a Packard, which she had been known to race at daring speeds as fast as seventy-five miles per hour. The *East Hampton Star* described her appearance in court: she was dressed in the latest fashion and wearing sparkling diamond rings on her fingers. Helen also came to the Amityville police station flashing $500 to bail out her brother Frank when he had been caught on the Motor Parkway when his car broke down while transporting a shipment of liquor.[111]

THE *FRANCIS P. RITCHIE* was an eighty-six-foot fishing smack owned by a reputed New York City bootlegger. Formerly a three-masted schooner, the smack had been converted into a speedboat when two large engines were installed, giving it the speed of ten knots per hour (eleven and a half miles per hour). The ship was anchored about fifteen miles off Shinnecock Light while the crew did a spot of fishing. The Coast Guard destroyer *Paulding*, which happened to be passing, decided that the ship—despite its innocent-seeming activity—was suspicious. The suspicions were well founded—authorities found crates of whiskey stored between the *Ritchie*'s bulkheads and compartments. James P. O'Connell and Pete O'Riley, both of Manhattan, along with Jack Wallace of Mineola and John Veryzer of Islip were arrested.[112]

DOWN A LONELY ROAD in Calverton ambled a truck that had eluded a barrage of revenue agents who were watching Montauk Highway. The five-ton truck driven by Henry Potter and Joseph Coselli, both of Manhattan, had a cargo of seventy cases of rye, which was stored not in the usual glass bottles but in a never-before-seen series of five-gallon kegs.[113]

PATCHOGUE POLICE CAPTAIN WILLIAM H. Valentine must have radiated a sense of authority that affected all who surrounded him. As he was walking down the street in Patchogue, a car whizzed past him. Bellowing at the driver to stop the car brought instant results, as Joseph Powell of Islip jammed on the brakes and pulled over. Valentine, who merely wanted Powell to slow down, caught up with the car and probably intended to give the driver a lecture on the virtues of slowing down when in town. Then Valentine noticed that there was a blanket covering something in the back seat. Flipping up the blanket revealed twelve cases of liquor and Powell's arrest.[114]

AS THE GOVERNMENT AGENTS became better funded and wiser to the many tactics used by the smugglers across Long Island, the number of rumrunning and bootlegging cases began to drop. But that did not stop the vigilance of federal agents. Paramount Pictures was working on a new movie, *The Story Without a Name*, an Irvin Willat silent film.

The film crew and actors had rented a yacht and were cruising the waters of Long Island while rehearsing and filming. Louis Wolheim and Ivan Linow were hired to portray rough-looking tough guys. They were so good that revenue officers, who spotted them on deck, stopped and boarded the yacht. As they boarded, the government officials demanded the ship's paperwork. The director was quickly summoned and told the officers that the ship had only coal, movie cameras and the actors. "Cut that stuff," said the agents. "We'll search the boat for liquor. I don't like the looks of these two fellows." A finger of scorn was pointed at Wolheim and Linow, who had been letting their beards grow for a week so as to look rough."

At that moment, leading lady Agnes Ayres and her maid wandered out onto the deck to see what the excitement was. The government agents

Miss Agnes Ayres

Actress Agnes Ayres, one of the stars in a rumrunning film, *The Story Without a Name*, directed by Irving Willat. *From the* Long Islander, *September 8, 1922, page 13, and* Ogdensburg Republican Journal, *June 19, 1930, page 6.*

probably did a double take and realized that perhaps the men had been telling the truth. However, wanting to make sure that the occupants of the yacht weren't pulling an elaborate hoax, they decided to settle in and watch the actors film. Willat then called to his cameramen and gathered Antonio Moreno, the leading man, and Agnes Ayres to work on the next scene. The movie was released into theaters in 1925.[115]

1926

Hans Fuhrmann and his friends found not only an exciting way to make money, but they also had access to a lot of booze every time they went to work. Unfortunately for Hans, while he made a good salary, he was drinking his paycheck away as quickly as earned it. Besides, not everyone was happy being a part of the rumrunning business. Hans's wife, Annie L. Fuhrmann of Greenport, was more disgruntled than most because her husband often returned from his rumrunning voyages intoxicated and broke instead of bringing his pay home.

Rather than nag and argue with her husband about his habit of drinking his entire pay from each voyage, Mrs. Fuhrmann decided to go to the source. She contacted her husband's rumrunning bosses and demanded they give her at least part of her husband's salary instead of giving it all to him to drink away. Hans's employers "only laughed and said that was my funeral. Well, I want to make it their funeral, too."[116]

That summer, she learned that her husband, who had left for a three-month rumrunning voyage, had been arrested and was being held prisoner under an assumed name along with the rest of the crew on the steamer *Nantisco*. The ship and crew had been caught with $3,000 of Canadian alcohol near Astoria. Determined to free her husband from the grasp of the smugglers, she began to search for a way.

Annie Fuhrmann realized the best way to hurt the rumrunners was to hurt them financially, the same way she was hurt every time her husband drank his paycheck instead of bringing it home. But how could she, a regular citizen, get in touch with the proper authorities who could help her achieve her goal?

While most women were struggling to get the vote, Mabel Willebrandt rose to become a U.S. assistant attorney general in 1921. *Library of Congress.*

The best way to catch the attention of the high-powered government officials was, of course, to reach them through the newspapers. So she wrote to the Patchogue-area reporter for the *Brooklyn Daily Eagle*, asking for assistance in getting her plea to the right ears.

Soon the Prohibition Enforcement Bureau sent a special undercover investigator to hear Mrs. Furhmann's case. Then Mabel Willebrandt, the U.S. assistant attorney general, who was in charge of handling all Prohibition cases, became involved.

Annie Furhmann began to work closely with the government investigation, telling them all she knew about the operation. When she learned that her husband had been incarcerated for violating the Volstead Act, she closed up her house and moved temporarily to Brooklyn.

When she was reunited with her husband, he still had charges pending against him, which helped to convince him to help turn state's evidence. Furhmann began to tell everything he knew about the operations of his employers. Mrs. Furhmann had been present at several meetings that were held in her Greenport home when the smuggling leaders had used it as a temporary base to plan, hire and pay employees.

She provided authorities with names, addresses and a wealth of details. The government put her on payroll as a special investigator and paid for all of her living expenses for the time she spent in Brooklyn.

The information that the Furhmanns provided led to raids on the headquarters of the smuggling ring at the Longacre and Knickerbocker buildings in New York City and the surrender of the ring's leader, Arthur Krauss.

During the raid, Hans Fuhrmann stood with the group of officers. As each member of the syndicate was arrested, he was brought to the group and Fuhrmann identified him by name and occupation.[117] Six months later, Fuhrmann was found dead of a bullet to the head.[118] The murderer was never found.

NOT EVERY BOAT WAS seized red-handed in the battle between rumrunners and the federal authorities. The *Nora* of Greenport was sailing up Mattituck Creek when it was stopped and seized by Patrol Boat 127. Captain William De Wolf and his crew of three sailors were arrested. The *Nora* was taken into custody because state authorities claimed that they had information that

The Old Mill, located along Mattituck Creek, was never raided. It was a reputed speakeasy that had a trapdoor in its floor for unloading cargo. *Author's collection.*

linked the boat to rumrunning activities. When searched, the boat had not a drop of liquor on board; despite the lack of evidence, the ship and crew were brought up to New York City for questioning.[119]

———— ∞∞∞ ————

As the smuggling business got bigger and bigger, more and more ruthless people joined the ranks in the struggle to control the profits. Stories began to circulate of fishermen and crews on Rum Row being hijacked and held prisoner. William Greerer of Brooklyn had come out to the North Fork for a relaxing summer vacation in Greenport. One day as he strolled the beaches on the sound shore between East Marion and Orient, he picked up bottle that had floated up to the beach. Holding the bottle up to the light, Greerer noticed something inside.

Written on a torn piece of paper from a notebook was a message: "Help Am prisoner on rum ship James III off Block Island. Was taken prisoner yesterday night while fishing. Please notify some government official that the ship is sending in stuff all time by speed boats. There's about two aliens ready to be brought ashore. Send help immediately, Thanks Walters. P.S.— My Boat was sailed away by one of the crew." On the reverse of the note was printed, "Help Needed." The note, found in July, was dated May 12.[120]

1927

Nine men, five trucks and 650 cases of Canadian Club whiskey and champagne made the day of the Bay Shore office of New York State Troopers in the spring of 1927. Anthony Bonaventure, Michael Bruino, John Kelly, Vincent Salafain and Joseph Diminico of New York City; Michael Chunco and John Smith of Huntington; and Albert F. Dion of Patchogue along with DeWitt Lawson of Montauk were all found red-handed by Trooper L.F. McLaughlin, who was on the hunt for overloaded trucks on a crack of dawn Tuesday assignment. Rumor had it that McLaughlin was responding to a tip given by two rival Patchogue bootleggers. At six o'clock in the morning near Canoe Place Inn in Hampton Bays, the first of the heavily laden trucks rumbled down the road. McLaughlin detained the truck and began looking it over. Discovering the crates of whiskey, the trooper arrested the driver and quickly learned that more trucks were on their way. Running for a telephone, he called the trooper barracks in Bay Shore and requested reinforcements.

A fleet of pleasure cars began making their way down the road, and they were soon stopped and inspected. Fifteen drivers were also placed under arrest. By the time the detachment of state troopers arrived, more of the rum trucks had begun appearing. One truck after another was stopped, searched and the drivers and helpers arrested. An additional five liquor-toting drivers were also discovered before authorities called it a day.

The troopers, after seizing the trucks and questioning their prisoners, sent reinforcements out to Montauk, where they found the rumrunning vessel still tied up to the dock at Fort Pond Bay with sixty-three cases on

Being the first landfall a ship could reach on Long Island made landing cargo in Montauk attractive to rumrunners. *Courtesy of the Oysterponds Historical Society, Orient, New York.*

board. The operation at the shoreline was as well-equipped and efficient as any other commercial business. A narrow-gauge railroad had been built from the dock to a warehouse where the liquor was stored until it was ready to be shipped by truck.

The boat, captained by DeWitt Lawson of Montauk, was reputed to have been seen off of Montauk Point and Ditch Plains for the previous two days. It was 110 feet long and fast. Rumor said the boat had engine trouble and was towed into Fort Pond Bay, where it offloaded its cargo. The smugglers must have been having a bad night, because after having boat trouble, they found that they needed another truck. So a local trucking company was called and told a story. The trucking company was informed that a truck had broken down on the side of the road between Southampton and Bridgehampton and the cargo needed to be rescued and delivered. When the driver from the trucking company arrived, instead of finding a stranded truck, he was told to go on to Amagansett. Realizing that perhaps this job wasn't on the up-and-up, he began to try to back out but was told that the owner knew what was going on and had okayed the trip. When he arrived at Amagansett, the driver discovered that he had landed in the middle of a bootlegging trip. He later claimed that the cargo was loaded onto his truck against his wishes and that he was ordered to lead the fleet.

The two Patchogue bootleggers, who may have tipped off federal agents about the operation, were at the Amagansett loading site with their car.

The east side of Fort Pond Bay in Montauk. The village was pretty much obliterated by the 1938 hurricane. *Courtesy of the Oysterponds Historical Society, Orient, New York.*

The pair had been negotiating to get the load of liquor that had been loaded into their car for free. When they were refused, they threatened the manager of the operation: either give them a truckload of booze or they would snitch to the troopers. When that failed to get the results they wanted, the pair drove off just before troopers arrived.[121]

One advantage rumrunners had was the availability of surplus, well-built military vessels. The *Anetta I*, a former submarine chaser, was one of many former military vessels pressed into service as a rumrunner. Some of the liquor captured by the state troopers by Canoe Place Inn in Hampton Bays was thought to have come ashore on the *Anetta I*. This was the third time that the boat had been seized by authorities. Each time the boat was sold at auction its "new" owner put it back into service as a rumrunner.[122]

Frederick Pitts of Sayville either made a good decision or a bad one, depending on how you look at it. At the trial of organized crime figures Edward and Frank Costello (as well as sixteen others), he admitted to double-crossing Detective A. Bruce Bielaski. Pitts, who had worked for the Costello crowd, quit when they refused to pay him money that he felt he was owed. Going to

Frank Costello, a lifelong criminal, was born in Italy and one of the few organized crime bosses to live a long life. *Library of Congress.*

work for the opposition, Pitts took a job as an informer for Bielaski for $45 a week. Seeing opportunity, Pitts offered to sell out Bielaski for the princely sum of $4,800. His admission got him sentenced to prison in the Tombs. This may have been a lighter punishment, since most organized crime figures, like Frank Costello, repaid men who double-crossed them with death.[123]

IN THE FALL OF 1927, there was an epidemic of cars being stolen across Long Island. So many had gone missing that police departments were considering making searching for them a separate job. Cars were disappearing from the back of businesses and homes and being found days later in the city with many miles added to the speedometer. The police suspected that the cars were being taken and used by the rumrunners. Citizens were advised to start locking their car doors.[124]

A rare local rumrunning photo from Quogue shows the local Coast Guard crew confiscating a recently captured haul of liquor on the beach. *Courtesy of the Quogue Historical Society, Quogue, New York.*

IT WAS A RACE between the residents of Quogue and Hampton Bays versus the Coast Guard in April 1927. In an effort to move faster by lightening their load, a rumrunner being chased by the Coast Guard had thrown case after case of scotch overboard. The cases riding the waves were estimated to be fifteen to twenty miles out, but they were floating toward the shore. Guardsmen from the Quogue station spotted the first crate floating inland, and by two o'clock in the afternoon, it had become a race—all the locals turned out determined to get a slice of the bounty floating toward their community before the government swept it all up.[125]

1928

It wasn't always the Coast Guard shooting at the rumrunners. Sometimes the rumrunners shot back! Guardsman William J. Hoolahan of the Quogue Coast Guard Station found this out in late in the fall of 1928. Hoolahan was walking on the beach in the dark east of the station when he heard a boat being pulled up onto the shore. After calling out, he was told to freeze or else. Disregarding the warning, Hoolahan began heading toward where he heard the voice. Suddenly a shot rang out, and he felt it hit him in his left leg. As he fell to the ground, Hoolahan pulled out his pistol and returned fire, scattering the rumrunners, who grabbed their boat and headed back out on to the water. Hoolahan was able to crawl to a nearby the telephone station and called his captain for help. Later the investigation reported that a beam trawler with an engine was seen leaving the area and heading west.[126]

WHEN YOU COMMIT A crime, it can spin into a bigger and bigger problem. William DeMarco was one of the owners of the Sinclair House in Amityville. He and his partner, Alfred D'Andrea, had a problem: while the men were selling illegal booze, they were also being blackmailed by Major E.C. Schroeder, who was the head of the industrial alcohol inspection section of the Prohibition office in New York. Looking to get out from under Schroeder's demands, D'Andrea turned evidence against their blackmailer.

While D'Andrea gave up the information on Schroeder, he also inadvertently implicated his partner. Schroeder got two years in jail and a $10,000 fine. DeMarco ended up serving five days in jail.[127]

—⊗⊗⊗—

IN LATE DECEMBER, SOME duck hunters were checking out their prospects on the edge of Round Pond, which sits just south of Sag Harbor. As the hunters surveyed the area, they were startled to spot a body swinging gently from a tree over the water. Racing over to the body, the men discovered it was an effigy, dressed in a slightly worn serge suit, complete with underwear, necktie, silk socks and a fashionable fedora.

Authorities, when notified, realized that no one in the area was reported missing and speculated that the effigy was a signal for a meeting place, bootleggers or a grisly practical joke. Local residents reported hearing a singing ghost most nights in the nearby cemetery, warbling an assortment of sailor songs, and the sounds of powerful trucks moving over Sagg Road toward Montauk Highway. Although groups were organized to try to catch the ghost, no one was ever spotted.[128]

1929

The forty-foot speedboat *Marjorie*, loaded with five hundred cases of champagne and whiskey, raced toward the entrance to Great Pond in Montauk, closely followed by Coast Guard Patrol Boat 124. The *Marjorie* was spotted at dawn just off the Great Pond area, and officials ordered the boat to stop for boarding. Instead, the boat accelerated and was starting to outpace the patrol boat when the Coast Guard captain ordered his crew to open fire with the machine gun that was mounted on the deck.

The rapid-fire gun quickly disabled the fleeing *Marjorie*, and the speedboat was grounded at the entrance to the harbor. Three guardsmen rowed over and found the decks piled with bags containing whiskey and champagne. Two of the rumrunning men, Sully Anderson and Henry Knowles of Halifax, Nova Scotia, surrendered immediately. The third man, J.E. Stevens of New York City, who was attempting to escape, stopped when officials fired at him as he was disappearing into the surrounding underbrush. The three men were arrested and taken into custody.[129]

TWO VESSELS WERE HOVERING off the coast: the *Flor del Mal*, a British converted submarine chaser, and *Roamer*, a fishing sloop. During the day, they stayed between 150 to 200 miles offshore; at night they moved closer in, to between 20 to 50 miles off Long Island. For two weeks, these large vessels moved back and forth. Their travels caught the eye of the Coast Guard, which assigned

Fort Pond Bay   Montauk, Long Island, N. Y.

Crew of Rum Vessels Captured by Guard

CAPTURED OFF MONTAUK POINT when two rum-running boats were seized, fifteen crew members were escorted by Coast Guardsmen. Prisoners are shown being taken to barge office for questioning. Liquor taken was worth $100,000.

Above: Montauk originally huddled between Fort Pond Bay and the Atlantic Ocean. The community was moved in the 1940s by the military to its current site. *Courtesy of the Oysterponds Historical Society, Orient, New York.*

Left: Captured off Montauk, the crew of a rumrunner file off the ship under the watchful eye of the Coast Guard. *From the* Patchogue Advance, *March 21, 1930, page 9.*

a patrol boat to monitor their movements. Coast Guard captain Randolph Ridgley worried that the ships were equipped with the latest in technology—the radio. He was also fairly certain that the ships had landed cargo valued at more than $1 million a week earlier in Glen Cove and Fort Pond Bay. Captain Ridgley wanted these ships. Just a couple of hours after Captain Ridgley gave his statement, the Coast Guard was hard at work chasing one of the rum boats racing to shore by Newport. As the rumrunners were unwilling to stop when ordered, the guards opened fire and killed three of the crew and wounded a fourth member. The second boat was captured off Montauk and a third seized as it was entering into Napeague Bay.

Determined to capture the larger ships if they strayed into U.S. waters during their wanderings in and out of the area, the authorities waited. Finally, the *Flor del Mal* was spotted off Shagwong Reef near Montauk. The *Legare* approached the ship and demanded that the crew identify themselves. The *Flor del Mal* ignored them. Moving in closer to repeat the demand, the guard realized that the ship was deserted and had been set on fire. The guardsmen discovered the ship's crew had escaped in the smaller lifeboats that were missing from the ship. The Coast Guard managed to put out the fire and towed the ship into port. A search of the ship revealed that it still had four thousand cases stashed aboard.[130]

THE FISHING SHIP *ROAMER* was captured when it sailed into Napeague Bay, not realizing that a patrol boat was lurking nearby. Nearby spotters, realizing that the patrol boat was closing in on its prey, gave the signal to the crew to abandon ship. The crew quickly evacuated to the shore and disappeared inland, leaving behind the *Roamer* and five hundred cases of liquor.[131]

EARLY ON A DECEMBER morning, Patchogue awoke to the sounds of a gun battle playing out at the foot of Underwood Street. Rumrunners were determined to land their boat load of liquor on a dock near George Bishop's shipyard. The police were equally determined to stop them. Two trucks to carry the liquor and a crew of approximately forty men to transfer the load were all waiting for the rumrunning boat to dock.

At two o'clock in the morning, Officers William Kordes and James Dutcher along with Constable William Arnold of Blue Point got a tip that two trucks were being loaded with booze. However, when the officials arrived at the scene, the boat carrying the liquor had not yet docked. Spotting the cops, the waiting men scattered as fast as they could. Calling for the men to halt, the officers discharged their weapons at the fleeing men. Two men unable to reach the safety of the local streets fast enough dove into the chilly waters and swam away.

Kordes, Dutcher and Arnold seized the trucks and placed the drivers under arrest. The boat crew, seeing the waiting men dashing away, realized that they were sailing into a trap and reversed course to the middle of the river. The vessel started drifting south toward an alternate unload site.[132]

FRANK RICKERS OF NEW York City was reputed to be running large loads of booze through the West Islip area. Two hundred bags of alcohol stuffed into a truck and a car were seized and six men arrested when Coast Guard officials pounced on the men as they were busy transferring the bags at the foot of Snedecor Avenue in West Islip. The liquor was brought into the village the night before and scheduled to be delivered in Brooklyn.[133]

WALTER NEVINS, FRANK RIKERS, Frank Bruno, Frank Fanio, Harry Cohen and Herman Sobel, all of New York City, were having a really bad day. Their truck carrying a $10,000 load of liquor not only got stuck in the mud alongside a creek at the foot of Snedecor Avenue in West Islip but the driveshaft had broken when the men tried to get the vehicle out of the mud as well. To put the icing on the cake, as they were trying to fix the driveshaft so they could get their delivery on the road, someone called

Glass and liquid weigh a lot. One way police could spot an inexperienced bootlegger was to look for a car that had a sagging suspension. *Library of Congress.*

the sheriff's department on them. Deputy Sheriffs William J. Hunt and Charles Barcellona quickly took the unlucky men and the truck of booze into custody.[134]

IN AN EFFORT TO break the largest rumrunning syndicate on the East Coast, federal agents simultaneously raided thirty-five sites along a two-hundred-mile stretch of coastline in October 1929. The sites raided stretched from Atlantic Highlands, New Jersey, to Sag Harbor. Included in the raids was the syndicate's headquarters, located in the former mansion of Oscar Hammerstein Jr. The million-dollar smuggling ring's directors were arrested in the raids, and an unlicensed radio and a batch of machine guns were also captured.[135]

1930

Men in the rumrunning business put their lives on the line for profit. Those who were caught knew to keep their mouths shut—after the smugglers were caught, the worst the Feds could do would be to put them in jail. On the other hand, if they talked, their bosses would find a more permanent way to punish them, as Hans Fuhrmann found out. In 1930, the crew of the British ship *Eleanor Joan* was caught hauling 2,800 sacks of liquor from St. Pierre, Canada. The ship, which was spotted by the Coast Guard patrol boat 289, was traveling past Plum Gut on its way toward Greenport. The twelve-foot *Eleanor Jane* had a crew of eight men from Halifax and one American from Manhattan. The ship, which had a powerful gas engine, ignored the patrol boat when it fired its first blank shot. It wasn't until Patrol Boat 289 began to use live ammunition that the ship slowed and then attempted to ram the Coast Guard boat. The *Eleanor Jane* was quickly taken into custody, and the crew was eventually sentenced to jail.[136]

ON THE EDGE OF Southold Town's border, just off Dumpling Lighthouse, the Patrol Boat 290 spotted a rumrunner, the *Black Duck*, preparing to land its cargo of five hundred cases near Newport, Rhode Island. Officials ordered the vessel to stop and were ignored by the four men crewing one of the fastest boats in the area. The patrol boat then opened fire with its machine gun to stop the fleeing vessel. Raked with a hail of deadly bullets, the runner came to a halt. The Coast Guard's shots had killed three of the four men onboard. The ship was towed to Providence, Rhode Island, and a grand jury was convened to consider the evidence in the case. It acquitted the crew of Patrol Boat 290. The *Black Duck* was impounded, repaired and added to the Coast Guard's fleet. The case helped to cement government officials' status as "untouchable" while performing their duties in the war against liquor.[137]

Not even James Hildreth, superintendent of the Bureau of Marine Fisheries, was safe from the roving patrols along the beaches of the South Fork. Hildreth and his wife were part of a group returning from a dance held at the Fort Pond Bay restaurant by the Montauk Square Club. As the group drove their cars along the road by Napeague Beach at four o'clock on a Saturday morning in February, Hildreth noticed several men in the road and then several flashes of light before the quiet of the morning was suddenly broken by a volley of gunshots. Startled, he stopped the car as the men approached.

Recognizing the men were in Coast Guard uniform, Hildreth asked who was in charge. One of the men volunteered that he was Captain Warner; when Hildreth asked if he could prove he was in charge, the man stuck out his arm and silently pointed to the chevrons on his sleeve. The conversation between the two men on whether the Coast Guard had the right to stop civilian cars, especially with a volley of gunshots, became heated. William Young, who was one of the drivers, realized that Hildreth and Warner were well on their way to blows, stepped between the men and managed to de-escalate the argument.

Apparently, Captain Frank D. Warner's patrol, spying the group, decided that the line of cars so early in the morning was suspicious. After peeking into the cars, Warner offered no explanation for stopping them. He merely said he was sorry and would have liked to have gone to the dance too, before telling the drivers that they could go. Hildreth, indignant, complained to District Attorney Alexander Blue about the incident.

The complaint was brought to court in Riverhead. Captain Warner, a twenty-eight-year veteran with the Coast Guard, informed the court that according to his orders from his superior officer Commander Sullivan, the Coast Guard had been given the power to stop automobiles on public highways of the state as of late January 1930 because of the sheer quantity of liquor flowing from the South Shore and the inability of authorities to stop the pipeline. Warner, who was in charge of the stations at Hither Plains, Napeague Beach and Ditch Plains, admitted that the Coast Guard with its current manpower and equipment was unable, despite its best efforts to completely stop the smuggling.[138]

---∞∞∞---

THE RESIDENTS OF THE East End learned from the cradle to never let opportunity pass them by. As the smugglers and government wrestled over possession of the liquor being brought ashore and transported, residents quietly scooped up and took home bottles that were abandoned by either side.

In February 1930, the Coast Guard got a call that a beam trawler was in distress by the South Fork's Oyster Pond. Coast Guard captain Frank Warner immediately went to investigate. The ship, with Adolph Steinfelt, the owner and captain, onboard was beached in about four feet of water. After searching the ship, Warner found it to be empty of any illegal cargo. A suspicious man, Warner decided to arrest Steinfelt anyway, called to New London to have the *Notus* taken into custody and towed the ship into port. By late afternoon, two Coast Guard ships, the *Eagle* and *Nimaha*, had arrived. The crew from the *Eagle* were soon set to work in the freezing water, searching for the cargo that Warner was sure had been on the *Notus*.

Soon the men began bringing up liquor, bags of it. A total of 330 out of an estimated 400 sacks were found and brought to shore. As word of the Coast Guard men searching the waters spread, crowds of residents armed with clam rakes, eel spears and nets began to appear along the roadway, all ready to search for some of the cargo from the beached ship.

As residents began to approach the beach, all set to collect what they could, the Coast Guard patrol turned their guns on the locals. William Petty, who was among the crowd, along with Richard Bennett, Kenneth King, Arnold Hulse and Al Garrow, recalled that the officer of the patrol said as the Coast Guard men got into a boat, "'You people get behind the bank and stay there. We're leaving and we're going to spray the shore with machine gunfire if you move.' 'We thought he was bluffing,' said Petty, 'so we ran down to the beach. All of a sudden there was a noise like a lot of hornets and sand and water began spitting up. We got out of there quick.'"[139] Anyone, including the curiosity seekers, who attempted to move past the hills of the beach toward the water was shot at.

This quickly brought complaints from the crowd to the sheriff's department. When Deputy Sheriff John P. Jenson and E.C. Morford found and spoke to the Coast Guard official who was in charge of the ships about the shootings, the officer declined to comment. The Coast Guard, like the Prohibition agents, were, in a word, untouchable when they were enforcing the Volstead Act. The only action the deputies could and did take was to report the incident to District Attorney Alexander Blue. The incident was brought to court, and after hearing the testimony of a number of people who were involved, Justice Leek could only express his feelings. He condemned not only the incident but also "the practice of stopping pleasure cars on the public highways...without reasonable cause to believe that they are in an illegal transaction."[140]

A HEAVY FOG BLANKETED the coast one week in the fall of 1930. The system stretched from Maine to Delaware and wreaked havoc with the maritime industry on the eastern end of Long Island. The *Harry Bowen*, carrying tons of coal heading for New Bedford, Massachusetts, crashed into the rocks at Ditch Plains. The weather had also caused four other vessels in the area to wreck, including the fifty-foot *Winifred H.*, a fishing sloop, which ran ashore on the beach at Napeague in the heavy fog. The crew unloaded 1,100 cases of whiskey on the beach as they tried to refloat the boat. Unfortunately for the smugglers, the Coast Guard discovered the *Winifred H.* and its cargo. While the crew got away, they left everything behind. It took the better part of a week for the Coast Guard to free up enough men to get the ship refloated; meanwhile, cases and bags of whiskey were floating up on to shore. Locals took advantage of the officials' distraction, pulled on their hip boots and spent time searching for the *Winifred H.*'s cargo.[141]

This was the second time the *Winifred H.* of Sayville had come to the attention of authorities. The ship, which was owned by Ivanhoe Stein of Sayville and captained by William DeWall of Greenport, had run afoul of the law in June 1930, when DeWall, Nick Swartz of Patchogue, William Johnson of Blue Point, James Linden of Greenport and Arthur Woods of Brooklyn were caught alongside the *Winifred H.* with a tractor hauling nine hundred cases of rye and bourbon down the beach away from the sloop.[142]

EARLY ON A SUNDAY morning on a beach opposite Patchogue, four men using tractors and trailers, were captured by Ellis Gray from the Blue Point Coast Guard Station. The men were hauling cargo across the barrier beach to the bay to reload it on another boat for its trip into the Patchogue area. Gray, who had been doing a routine patrol, happened across the operation. When he spotted the men, he quickly summoned backup from the station before confronting the workers. Apparently, the four men were part of a larger fifteen-man group of locals working to unload and reload the cargo from a boat to a tractor and trailer, then back onto another boat. All of the men except for the unlucky four slipped away in their boats when Gray and his fellow guardsmen appeared. Reports on the size of the cargo ranged from 35 cases to 250 cases.[143]

THE FISHING SCHOONER *LIBERTY* of Sag Harbor was making its way along the shore on the south side of Montauk Point when Patrol Boat 289 suddenly appeared. After boarding, Coast Guard officials discovered six hundred sacks of liquor, seized the ship and arrested the crew of four men.[144]

THANKSGIVING AND THE HOLIDAYS were the busy season for the rumrunners and the Coast Guard. In 1930, there was a definite uptick in the activity of the smugglers due to a new Canadian export act, which slowed traffic on the Detroit River and diverted more liquor shipments to the East Coast. The speedboat *Desiree*, hoping to avoid detection, was running without lights on a moonless night in late October, trying in vain to slip past the Coast Guard's picket boats. Authorities, who were actually searching for a supply ship, spotted the *Desiree* and fired warning shots. The *Desiree*, rather than risk death, slowed to a halt and was taken into custody; five other vessels were captured within the next thirty-six hours.[145]

SOME BOATS WERE BETTER had hiding than others—the sixty-five-foot *Helen* out of New York was just such a craft. Like the *Desiree*, the *Helen* was running at night with its lights out when it blundered into a group of Coast Guard vessels. After ignoring the warning shot from a cannon and dodging a hail of bullets from the machine guns, the *Helen* managed to outdistance the official's ships and was skirting Gardiners Island when it ran aground. It took three days of hunting for the Coast Guard to find and capture the elusive vessel and its cargo of six hundred sacks; however, the crew escaped the grasp of the authorities.[146]

RUNNING AGROUND WHEN BEING chased by the Coast Guard so the crew could escape was becoming more and more common. Racing across the waves, the *Mary B.* flew just off Montauk Point, hotly pursued by a Coast Guard patrol boat. After a five-mile chase, the crew grounded the boat and fled inland, escaping officials and leaving behind three hundred cases of ale and scotch.[147]

IT WASN'T ONLY THE small speedboats the Coast Guard was after: when a supply ship strayed into U.S. territorial waters, it was also subject to search and seizure. The *Paul Jones*, a trawler, was pretty well known by the Coast Guard. When it was spotted near Fire Island, the guardsmen must have thought

U. S. COAST GUARD STATION NO. 84, OAK BEACH, N. Y.

Built as a lifesaving station, the Oak Beach Coast Guard Station is today the town of Babylon's Oak Beach Community Center. *Courtesy of Town of Babylon, Office of Historic Services.*

it was their lucky day. The ship was apparently waiting for a speedboat to come and pick up its cargo. Leaping into action, the Coast Guard crew fired several shots across the trawler's bow. Instead of turning away, the ship began to move as quickly as it could toward shore. The Coast Guard fired a second set of shots as the crew of the *Paul Jones* leaped overboard and struck out for the beach. By the time the patrol boat pulled up alongside the ship and got it under control, they discovered that there was not a soul on board; the entire crew had escaped.[148]

A COMMON SIGHT ON the East End is the potato truck, piled high with potatoes. As the potato is a major crop on Long Island, in the fall, these trucks are ubiquitous. However, a potato truck driving quickly, with a large car packed with men following closely behind, is not as common. At least that is what William C. Nolan, C.B. Carter, C.M. Forbes, M. Raincones and District Attorney Blue thought as the truck and car blew past them as they drove along a back road from East Moriches to Eastport. Realizing that the car was following the lumbering truck instead of trying to pass it and was keeping pace was enough for the carload of enforcement officials to make a U-turn and begin to chase the pair of vehicles.

As the officials began to overtake the car and truck, the men in the car following the potato truck realized that trouble was coming up behind them fast. The car suddenly pulled out, zipped around the truck and disappeared down the road.

The truck, driven by Lawrence John Geiger of Water Mill and his assistant Jack Brown of the Bronx, was pulled over. At first appearance, the truck was filled with small potatoes, but tucked under the potatoes were 250 to 300 cases of assorted liquors that may have come in from a similar load that was seized three weeks earlier by officials.[149]

A RAID BY FEDERAL agents at Orowoc Creek near Islip surprised a large gang that had just started unloading barrels of malt from a sixty-foot cruiser onto two trucks. The creeks around the Islip area had long been a problem location for government agents, who usually missed the bootleggers by arriving too early or too late to make an arrest. This time, however, the timing was perfect. Alexander Baris of Medford and his high-powered car were scooped up along with the boat, both trucks and ten men. The cargo and vehicles were worth an estimated $150,000.[150]

IT WAS NO SECRET that bootlegging and rumrunning were mostly controlled by gangs, which eventually formed into today's organized crime. While many of the leading figures in these gangs, such as Jack Diamond or Dutch Schultz, have become infamous over the years, one man, Charles "Vannie" Higgins, was just as violent but never became as well known. Higgins, a close friend of Jack Diamond, was reputed to be in charge of Diamond's liquor import business. Their territory grew to encompass most of the south shore.

In friendly competition with them was Leo Steinberg, a young man of means. Steinberg had run some of his liquor loads into areas that Higgins considered part of his territory. The two men met several times at the home of W. Clifford Wilson in Patchogue. Higgins wanted a cut of Steinberg's profits for the use of the area. When Steinberg refused, Higgins continued to demand payment. It was reported that Higgins not only met with Steinburg but also called him several times. Finally, on September 27, 1930, Higgins's patience ran out, and Leo Steinberg disappeared and was never seen again. It was thought that Steinberg was kidnapped by Vannie Higgins because he

BIRD'S EYE VIEW OF PECONIC RIVER, RIVERHEAD. L. I

Riverhead was the site of the county courthouse, and the place where those arrested were imprisoned and brought to trial in Suffolk County. *Author's collection.*

was last seen getting into Higgins's car after supervising the unloading of a large haul of booze. Rumor said that Higgins had established distribution sites in Port Jefferson and in Riverhead for their beer business.[151]

———∞∞∞———

IT WAS A PARADE! A parade of trucks that ran through Patchogue at three o'clock in the morning on the first Saturday in March. The cavalcade of trucks led by two fast cars quietly made its way across Roe Boulevard to Waverly Avenue and then north to Middle Country Road. The trucks were part of a group of New Jersey rumrunners moving their concealed caches of booze that had been hidden all over the Patchogue area. The group, which had been frustrated by authorities' close attention on the area and its traffic had decided to use the recent spate of foggy nights to move their cargo to its destination. Prohibition agents had suspected the existence of the caches but had been unable to find them despite several searches. Unfortunately for the Jersey gang, they were caught by officials before they left the community.[152]

———∞∞∞———

OWNING WATERFRONT PROPERTY NEAR a dock was not as pleasurable as you might imagine. John Crampton and his family had their home on the water near Bishops dock in Patchogue. For months, the Cramptons had been working hard to ignore the regular nighttime deliveries made to the dock by the house. Then in December the police got a tip-off about a cargo and stopped one of the waterborne deliveries. A short while later, on New Year's Eve, Crampton, who was entering his yard after a late night, was surprised when two men with guns appeared and ordered him to leave and not come back for a while. Crampton, noticing a boat docked near the shore, said that he just wanted to get into his house.

Five days later, another large boat appeared and men swarmed around his property. Hunkering down in the house, Crampton and his family worked hard at not seeing anything, even though they recognized some of the local men. But the gang was taking no chances: the phone lines to the house were cut, and a day or two later, the family received an envelope posted from New York City.

Inside was a newspaper clipping of an article about a bombing that occurred in New Haven, Connecticut, at the home of a suspected federal informant. In the margin, written in blood, was the message that Crampton would also get a "pineapple" (bomb) and to keep his mouth shut.

Frightened and distressed with the threats, Crampton quickly packed his family off to stay elsewhere. He then went to the police and the district attorney's office to plead for protection and assistance in ending the situation.[153] The situation must have been resolved, because not another word was written about Crampton or his family.

DESPITE HAVING THE MAJORITY of the attention of federal authorities focused on the East End and south shore of Long Island, rumrunners were still trying to land large loads. In February 1930, on a foggy Saturday morning, two rum vessels with cargos worth $150,000 were captured by the Coast Guard. Both a supply ship, the *Isabel H* of Britain, which had drifted inside the U.S. territorial waters, and one of the fast rum boats, the *Mohawk*, were surprised by the Coast Guard suddenly appearing out of the fog as the *Isabel H* was loading twenty-four thousand bottles onto the *Mohawk*. The crews of both vessels surrendered quietly, knowing there was no way to escape.[154]

No pictures exist of local captures of stills. Not surprisingly, rumrunners and bootleggers refrained from taking photos of their illegal activities. *Library of Congress.*

WHILE MOST OF THE alcohol that was captured and reported in the newspapers on Long Island came by ship from other countries, federal agent Wilbur was in Huntington when he received a tip that not far from the commercial district of the community there was a garage on Wall Street that had a large still set up. Gathering up Deputy Sheriff Amza Biggs and his officers, the authorities quietly approached the suspected site, surprising three men who were operating a huge distilling plant. A crew of Prohibition wreckers were dispatched to dismantle the two-thousand-gallon still and destroy the rest of the plant. Forty-eight barrels of booze found in the basement of an adjacent house were emptied by authorities while cans of liquor waiting to be shipped were taken by officials as evidence. Angelo Uliano, the owner of the properties and five other men connected to the operation were arrested.[155]

In order to maximize profits, not all liquor was smuggled into the country in drinkable form. Often the liquor had to be cut with water to lower the alcohol content to drinkable levels. Early in April 1930, the seizure of two rum speedboats loaded with $100,000 in an assortment of uncut cargo was a prize for federal agents. At the same time, in New York City, a conference of top officials was discussing the next steps in fighting the illegal importation problem in the area. To put pressure on the smuggling syndicates, authorities began to increase the manpower stationed in problem areas, such as Patchogue, which had seven deputy sheriffs assigned to the area. The new strategy appeared to be working, because the *Patchogue Advance* reported, "Leaders whom the liquor was intended for frankly stated that they 'were pulling out of Long Island for good,' as things were too unhealthy for them."[156] The attack on the syndicates was twofold: more and more of their illegal cargo was being discovered and seized, and the price of taking bribes from the smugglers was becoming too high for most in places of authority to even consider. After paying for months, rumrunners bribing officials to look the other way was starting to come to a close.[157]

DISTRICT ATTORNEY ALEXANDER BLUE enjoyed getting out into the field periodically. He was with an official group investigating what conditions were like, when near Eastport, the group was passed by Lawrence John Geiger of Water Mill and John Brown from the Bronx. The pair were driving a truck that had been reported as possibly being involved in transporting liquor. When the truck was inspected, it was, of course, packed with three hundred cases of liquor.[158]

On Middle Island Road near Coram, Deputy Sheriff John M. Harding was searching for an almost new Larrabee truck that had "Long Island Produce Co. Patchogue, L.I." painted on its side. The truck, which had a tarpaulin covering its contents, wasn't carrying produce but had been loaded with 250 sacks of booze destined for New York City. The driver, Meyer Weintroup, and his assistant, Samuel Joseph, both of New York City, told Harding when he stopped the truck and arrested the men that it was owned by Samuel Jaffe of New York.[159]

Barton Avenue in Patchogue sat a relatively new house—it was situated in the woods, just about two blocks east of Medford Avenue. Over time, the house began emanating a strong odor—the scent of fermentation and hops. The smell was enough that the house was placed under surveillance by Prohibition agents. By June 1930, officials felt that they had enough probable evidence to get a search warrant and sent in officers to investigate.

The house had been converted into a distillery for the production and bottling of beer. Six fifty-five-gallon vats cooked and fermented the brew. In the cellar were six metal drums each holding fifty-five gallons of beer waiting to be bottled. There was also a bottling operation set up in the cellar.

When investigators arrived, the house was deserted; the brewers had apparently been tipped off and escaped. The officials took charge of the 114 cases of beer waiting to be shipped and not only destroyed the beer but also dismantled the distillery on site. A second brewery run by George Sokop on Division Street in Patchogue was also found and destroyed.[160]

Early on a Friday morning, the Coast Guard spotted two yachts, the *Harmony* and the *Commodore*, traveling together heading toward the shore. When ordered to stop, the ships ignored the call until a hail of bullets from the government's guns persuaded them to halt.

Upon stopping and searching the yachts, authorities discovered two thousand sacks of uncut liquor, worth close to $100,000. On board the ships were John Broere of West Sayville, John Heyboer of Sayville and W.S. Wilson of Bay Shore, as well as eight other men. This was not the first time the Coast Guard had captured the men and their cargos. Hoping to avoid the stiffer penalties for being a repeat offender, Broere on the *Harmony* gave his name as Julian Broere of Newark, New Jersey. Heyboer claimed to be John Davis of Fort Pond Bay, and Wilson said his name was Lewis. Unfortunately for the men, their attempt to slip under the radar as repeat offenders failed.[161] After pleading guilty, the rumrunners were given a suspended sentenced, except for Broere, who received sixty days in federal prison, and Lewis (Wilson), who received a thirty-day sentence.[162]

PART OF WHAT MADE the smuggling gangs so successful was the radio. Practical transmitters and receivers were in use by 1900, and powerful radio stations

John A. Wilbur, C.M Bernstein, W. Patten and F. Redfern with the guns and radios seized at the Horton estate. *Courtesy of the Henry L. Ferguson Museum Collection.*

were hidden in homes along the shoreline in eastern Suffolk. The radios were not lightweight. In 1930, Prohibition agents found and seized three radio stations run by rumrunners. Each of the radios weighed one ton, and they were estimated to be worth more than $6,000 a piece.

One transmitter was traced to the Howard home in Southampton. E.J. Blake, Robert Vernocke and Alonzo M. Campbell, all of whom were at the house, were arrested. Another was found at the Horton mansion in Hampton Bays, hidden in a trunk stored in the garage, with garbage heaped on it. The radio had a remote-control unit, which was found in the billiard room of the mansion.

The third radio was discovered in a rented estate along Montauk Highway in Quogue. Joseph Wichert, who was a retired shoe manufacturer, had rented the site and was having a dinner party. He had pulled out the stops to impress his dinner guests. Wichert hired a local storekeeper, Peter Wyckoff, who also worked part time for Wichert, to act as his butler for the evening. Sam Schwartz of the Bronx was attempting to leave the property with a lady companion as the agents pulled in to raid the estate; he was immediately detained. As the agents burst into the building, not only did they surprise Wichert and his dinner guests, but they also discovered Patrick Fitzgerald of New York City with the radio receiving a message over the airwaves. Rather than disrupt the party, the Prohibition agents allowed Wichert and his guests to finish. Officials allowed the dinner guests to leave but arrested Wichert, Wyckoff and Schwartz for operating a radio without a license and "conspiracy to violate radio law." Fitzgerald was found to have already been under indictment for violation of the Volstead Act.[163]

Regular Republican
Nomination for

District Attorney

ALEXANDER G. BLUE
DESERVES
PROMOTION

Born in Patterson, New Jersey, Alexander Blue moved to Suffolk County in 1904. He was elected to the chief prosecutor's job in 1930. *From the* Patchogue Advance, *October 15, 1929, page 5.*

JUST BEFORE MIDNIGHT ON a rainy, windy night, a Mack truck came down the road toward the corner of West Main Street and Waverly Avenue in Patchogue. Acting on a tip about heavy late-night traffic moving thorough the area, District Attorney Alexander G. Blue—along with Deputy Sheriff

John Davis, Constable John Harding, Joseph Arata from Blue's office as well as Special Deputy L.C. Harris—followed the truck through the community to the intersection, where they pulled it over. Otto Brucker of Hicksville, the driver of the truck, owned by Henry C. Brengel of Hickville, was immediately arrested. As Blue and his companions began looking over the truck, a Ford coupe roared up, and two men leaped out of the car and began questioning the officials about the situation. Their behavior and questions aroused the suspicions of Davis and Harding, who arrested Henry J. McKeon of Massapequa and Sam Lewis of Freeport. As it turns out, the truck had a load of four hundred cases of liquor, and the Ford had an additional fifteen cases. It was 1:30 a.m., and not wanting to deal with having to guard and transport the haul before having to destroy it, Blue made an executive decision and decided to start smashing the bottles immediately. He had the cases in the car transferred to the truck and began driving toward the village dump. Halfway to his destination, the heavy weight of the truck sank into the soft, muddy ground. At 3:00 a.m., the stormy night began to intensify. Unable to free the truck from the mud, Blue and his men gave up and decided that their duty to destroy the cargo was more important than keeping Patchogue clean and beautiful. They began unloading the cargo and smashing the liquor bottles on the side of the road in the pouring rain. It took almost five hours to pry open each case, remove the carefully packed bottles and smash the several types of rye, three varieties of scotch, two types of gin and cordials and brandies.

When the sun rose to the stench of booze and mounds of broken glass on the side of the road, local officials as well as federal Prohibition agents were a bit upset. The feds, unhappy with Blue's decisions, threatened to hold local and county officers personally responsible for the mess. Blue shot back that when government officials took control of the illegal cargos, the loads seldom arrived intact to the location in Brooklyn where they were destroyed. He also informed federal authorities that if they were so unhappy with his actions he would "desist from all enforcement measures here and pass the responsibility to the federal officials." When an unnamed spokesperson from the Prohibition department persisted in chiding Blue, stating that, "we want definite and concrete evidence that the seizure and destruction were actually carried out in good faith. How otherwise can we be certain that the contraband was destroyed and not sold or given to persons of pull?"[164] Blue exploded, pointing out that the government appeared to be more worried about the rights of the smugglers than with society. He went on to inform reporters that one of his officers turned down a bribe, ownership of almost the whole load in return for allowing the suspects to escape with just twenty cases. "If the government…inform[s] me that they do not desire the assistance of the authorities of this county…it will be a direct challenge as to whether the government sincerely desires to enforce the Prohibition law in Suffolk County."[165]

It's the prize rum-running story of the year but no one will actually admit having seen it for fear that he may be accused of having been slipped a few bottles for being blind…on Montauk Highway just beyond Blue Point Avenue early Saturday morning. A heavily laden truck of rum broke down, being one of a fleet of three. The other two went on their way.…Shortly another truck arrived on the scene, backed up to the rear of the one stalled, and then, without any interference, the load was transferred.[166]

WHAT IS MORE REFRESHING during the summer than a beer? The thirsty drinkers of the East End had no need to make do during the summer of 1930. At the tail end of the summer, a commercial brewery was discovered by Prohibition agents on the east shore of Fort Pond Bay near the south end of the inlet. Officials found not only 160 cases of beer ready to be shipped but also "13 half-barrels of beer. The equipment consisted of a large bottling machine, a pasteurizing outfit and three full vats with a capacity of 25 barrels each. The plant had its own electric generating outfit and an elaborate system of marine railways to haul its supplies up from the water's edge by means of an electrical motor." The site, owned by Howard Seaman, was deserted by the time authorities arrived. It was estimated that the brewery produced between 25 and 35 barrels a week and delivered to the entire East End.[167]

THE MONTAUK BREWERY WAS not the only homegrown beer-making site discovered by authorities that month. Another was located on Railroad Avenue and Laurel Street in Holbrook. Charles Franz's operation had fifty-five cases of beer all set for delivery as well as twelve ten-gallon crocks of mash fermenting, two cases of malt and hops and a bottle washer and capper. Fortunately for Franz, he had already disappeared before officials arrived.[168]

W. CLIFFORD WILSON WAS a rich man. He had plenty of money and a mansion on Bay Avenue and Marvin Street in Patchogue. He also had close ties with Charles Steinberg, a debarred lawyer from Manhattan, whom authorities had suspected of being the head of a multimillion-dollar smuggling operation. It was probably frustrating to know a large smuggling organization was operating under their noses, but to be unable to prove it.

After tailing various members of the gang for six months, agents, in an effort to break the ring, had radio experts trace the airwaves until they found coded messages being sent out from sites in Brooklyn, Manhattan and a house on Lakewood Street in Patchogue. It was, at last, a break they needed. Authorities knew that the gang was connected to ten boats, including the *Harmony, Commodore, Edith, Ark* and *K2284,* some of which they had managed to capture periodically and impound only to have the gang buy the boats back when they came up at auction.

When agents felt they had all the proof they needed to make charges stick, they sent agents out to quietly arrest Wilson and one of his associates, Edward Green, who was a dress manufacturer in New York City. They also rounded up Edwin Baker of Bay Shore, who was a former Coast Guard official; Anthony Minardi; and John Rossa and William Gordon of Patchogue, who were caught red-handed cutting liquor at the building on Lakewood Street. Also swept up were Philip Waters and Leonard Steinberg

Laid out around 1733, the Montauk Highway was originally called South Country Road and ran along the length of the south shore of Long Island. *Author's collection.*

of Long Beach and Solomon Coleman of Sayville. The group relied on radio messages to guide their deliveries, an operation so well organized that they were rarely caught.

Charles Steinberg was difficult for the federal agents to pin anything on. The government ended up suing Steinberg for $1,892,278.98 for income tax due on his bootlegging profits in 1921.[169]

THERE IS AN OLD rhyme that says, "For want of a nail a crown was lost." For Albert B. Goldblatt of Brooklyn, for want of a taillight a cargo was lost. In mid-September 1930, Bayport was the site of a terrible accident: two women were killed when their car crashed into a truck whose taillights were out. The truck was partly in the road, waiting in a line to get gas. Since the accident, area police targeted trucks with nonfunctioning taillights for tickets.

Goldblatt, who was parked on Montauk Highway at the bend between Eastport and East Moriches, was on his very first liquor run. His truck was loaded up with eighty cases of assorted liquors when the tire went flat. On an early Saturday morning, with his truck half on the road and half on the shoulder, Goldblatt got out of the truck, sat down in the roadway and began to fix his tire.

Deputy Sheriff Albert Kehlenbeck of Patchogue was patrolling the highway when he spotted Goldblatt. Noticing that the truck was partially still in the lane of traffic and that the taillight was out, he pulled up next to the truck. After Kehlenbeck pointed out that the taillight was out, Goldblatt claimed that it must have just happened, because it was functioning when he started out on his trip. As Kehlenbeck began to write out a ticket for the light, the breeze began to bring an odor to his nose. "What's that smell?" Kehlenbeck wondered. Goldblatt quickly replied that it was the scent of a special load of potatoes. The officer, skeptical of the answer, decided that potatoes usually do not smell like liquor and moved to the back of the truck.

Opening the back, Kehlenbeck found eighty bags of assorted liquor, some of which had broken. Faced with the evidence of his bootlegging, Goldblatt confessed that he had been out of work for the last nine months and was desperate for work. The smuggling ring promised him $75 for the trip and a permanent job if he was successful. Instead of a new career, Goldblatt ended up with a suspended sentence and $2,500 bail for illegal transportation.[170]

THE *SUFFOLK COUNTY NEWS* headlines screamed, "District Attorney and His Men in Gun Fight with Rum Runners." The *Patchogue Advance* capped its article with "Blue and Two Officers Fight Pistol Battle in Speeding Cars with Desperate Rum Runners." Despite District Attorney Alexander Blue's spat with the federal government over his last adventure in capturing bootleggers, he continued working in the field tracking and capturing violators of the Volstead Act. On Monday, November 24, before 2:30 a.m., Blue was roused from his bed by a message from two men he had hired to work undercover. Three trucks were going to be loaded early at the exclusive Timber Point Club in Great River.

Blue quickly began trying to gather deputies to confront the smugglers. Unsuccessful in reaching any of the law enforcement agents, Blue hopped into his car, got Deputy Sheriff Albert Kehlenbeck and drove to Sayville to pick up his assistant, attorney Joseph Arata. Accompanied by the two undercover agents, the five men made their way to Great River.

Stopping where the road intersected with the country club's driveway, Blue and his men could see the caravan led by a large sedan emerging onto the highway. Blue and his men stepped onto the road and ordered the caravan to stop. In response, the lead car gunned its engine and raced toward the men. The officer whistled and called out again to the car to stop. The driver instead aimed his vehicle at Blue and stomped harder on the accelerator.

Montauk Highway has always run as a local road through the heart of many of Suffolk County's communities on the south side of the island. *Author's collection.*

Realizing that the car meant to run him down, Blue jumped out of the way at the last moment. Behind the lead car was a second car, which aimed itself at the officer on the other side of the road. After the officer leaped out of the way, the two cars were quickly followed by a volley of shots and the three fully loaded trucks. Bringing up the rear was a third car that headed toward Arata and Kehlenbeck, who both sprang onto the running boards of the auto. Arata slammed a blackjack into the driver, gained control of the vehicle, managed to stop it and ordered the two men inside out.

Commandeering the automobile, Arata slid behind the wheel. Blue leaped into the front seat, and Kehlenbeck jumped into the back. The men roared off down Great River Road toward Montauk Highway in pursuit. Soon they overtook one of the trucks. The other vehicles in the caravan had disappeared.

Chasing after the truck, as it neared East Islip, the officials tried to head it off. Arata brought his car level with the driver, and Blue told the driver to pull over. Instead of stopping, the truck driver yanked on his steering wheel and tried to force the smaller vehicle off the road. Arata had to swerve quickly, just missing slamming into a tree.

Maneuvering behind the truck, another car with four or five men in it raced up behind the officials: "As it neared somebody onboard opened fire on Blue's car, three shots marking the start of the encounter. It bore down on Blue's car and, instead of passing swerved into the rear full force, crashing in the back."[171]

The cars briefly locked together before Arata, straining, managed to keep control of his vehicle. The officials raced down the road following the fleeing truck, closely followed by the smugglers' car. Again the gangsters opened fire. Whipping out their pistols, Blue and Kehlenbeck twisted around and leaned out the windows to return fire. As the group raced through East Islip and then through the main street of Islip, the gun battle continued.

Realizing that there was no way to win in the situation, Blue told Arata to pass the truck and get to Bay Shore, where they could try to get help. As they attempted to pass the truck again, the driver tried to force them off the road. As soon as the trio arrived in Bay Shore, Blue and Kehlenbeck dashed into the state police headquarters. As they ran up the walk, the smugglers' gunmen, who had followed them, raced past and sprayed the authorities with bullets as they went by.

After rounding up eight state troopers, the group headed back to Timber Point Country Club to try to pick up the trail of the murderous bootleggers. When they arrived, they found five men who admitted to being loaders and

The name Islip is from ancestral estate of William Nicoll who once owned most of the area. The name was adopted in 1802. *Photo courtesy of the Oysterponds Historical Society, Orient, New York.*

the two men whose car Blue and his group had commandeered. All seven were taken into custody, but they soon had to be released due to lack of evidence.

Left with almost nothing to show for his efforts, Blue turned to the one possible lead in his possession, the car. But he soon found out that the car had stolen license plates, ending any chance of tracking down the ring that had been so determined to stop him.[172]

AT A SHACK ON Whitman Avenue near Islip High School, a loading party was raided. A woman calling herself Mrs. Smith appeared at the troopers' headquarters in Bay Shore and reported that something odd was happening at a house near her home. Corporal Curran was sent to investigate and came back reporting that a truck was being loaded as the sun set.

When the officer wandered up to the busy men, one man detached himself from the group and flashed a badge and claimed to be Suffolk County deputy sheriff William Lindsey of Peconic. When asked about what was going on, Lindsey informed Curran that the liquor had been seized that morning and he was having it moved. Thinking that it was odd that a local deputy and not a state or federal official would be loading a truck with a group of civilians, Curran reported back to headquarters.

Hearing about the situation, District Attorney Alexander Blue sent two of his men to look into the situation further. Soon both troopers and Blue's two men arrived at the shack. The truck was almost fully loaded, and bags of potatoes were being piled in on top of and around the liquor crates.

Loaded on the truck was $50,000 of Piper Heidsick Champagne, Knickerbocker, Old Log Cabin and Golden Wedding Rye Whiskey. Lindsey, who was brought before Blue, said that he got a tip that a truckful of liquor had been seized by hijackers and if Lindsey wanted credit for its capture he had to get to Islip. The owner of the truck told the Prohibition officers that Lindsay had called him and asked for a truck to take the liquor to Blue's office. It was thought that the cargo came from a larger load that had slipped past authorities the week before.[173]

THE HOLIDAY RUSH TO stock up with illegal liquor was in full swing. Everyone was rushing to make deliveries. At eight o'clock in the morning, a large fruit and produce truck was heading westbound in Smithtown. Speeding down the road, the driver was forced to swerve to avoid colliding with a car driven by John Fairchild of Setauket. The truck driver overcorrected and ended up colliding with a traffic light pole. Realizing that the truck was damaged to the point it would have to be towed, the driver and his assistant scrambled out of the cab and were soon picked up by a car.

As the rumrunner's boats became faster, so too did the Coast Guard's. This speedboat was photographed patrolling near Fire Island Inlet. *Courtesy of Town of Babylon, Office of Historic Services.*

As soon as he saw what was in the truck, investigating officer Constable L'Hommedieu called Deputy Sheriff Bertram Walker of Huntington to the scene. On the truck was two hundred cases of scotch, Old Carnegie, Ainslie's Royal Edinburgh, rye, vermouth and champagne, all covered with a layer of potatoes. Officials soon transported the cargo up to the city for processing.

On their way back at seven o'clock that evening, as the officials traveled thorough Smithtown they approached the same intersection that had seen the truck accident in that morning. A car came barreling through the intersection, blowing through the red light. Instantly turning around and pursuing the car, the officers pulled the driver, John Marino of New York City, over. Marino, who did not have a driver's license, of course had a car full of booze. Deputies noted that it was the second car of the same make and model seized from a bootlegger in the last couple of weeks.[174]

⸺∞⸺

THE COAST GUARD PATROL boat *Cartigan* was hot on the chase of the *Shanlian*, which for the last two hours had danced just out of reach of the *Cartigan*. For twenty-five miles, the two boats raced. The *Cartigan* fired at the fleeing ship whenever it could get close enough. But the dogged Coast Guard refused to give up. Finally, when the two boats were off Fire Island, the *Shanlian* suddenly slowed enough that the C.W. Whitney, the boatswain of the *Cartigan*, was able to have his vessel ram into the rumrunner's bow.

Boarding the *Shanlian*, the Coast Guard crew discovered twelve rumrunners all sporting several weeks' worth of untrimmed whiskers. Captain John H. McKenna of the *Shanlian* refused to surrender and scratched his beard as he admitted that the *Cartigan* only caught them because his engine crew disobeyed his orders.

The crew of the *Shanlian* was unlike any the Coast Guard had ever captured before: all expensively dressed, one crew member refused to leave the boat until "he had packed his dinner suit which he said he would need during his 'shore leave.'"[175] The *Shanlian* alone was valued at $100,000 because of the large number of electrical devices that were discovered aboard in addition to the liquor.[176]

⸺∞⸺

SOMETIMES A LOAD OF potatoes is just that. One of the biggest crops on Long Island, the potato was often used to hide loads of liquor on the

111

back of trucks because farm trucks filled with them was so prevalent on the island. When a group of state troopers spotted a ten-ton truck one morning just before Christmas, they were sure they had found a big load of booze. Acting on a tip, the troopers spotted the truck creeping through a thick snowstorm between East Islip and Bay Shore. After the truck pulled over, the driver was told that they were going to search his cargo. "No they weren't, the driver replied at least not here but if they wanted to take him to headquarters to do the deed, he was willing." The troopers decided to take the truck and driver to headquarters. Upon arrival, they told the driver to unload the truck. "'Nothing doing,' he replied; the troopers were conducting the search." So the driver stood back as the troopers began unloading sixty bags of potatoes, each weighing one hundred pounds. When they finally realized that the truck was carrying nothing but potatoes, the troopers gave up, reloaded the truck and watched the driver move off with a cheery Merry Christmas.[177]

Ten years into Prohibition, Suffolk County was growing weary of the constant battles between the federal government and the smugglers. The county joined a growing list of communities across New York State voting to repeal the Eighteenth Amendment. By September 1930, all of Long Island, Queens and Kings Counties had begun clamoring for change.[178]

1931

On a quiet August night in 1931, the *Artemis* (pronounced Art-Tee-mus)—a fast speed boat from Greenport—was sighted by the Coast Guard off Orient Point at midnight. The *Artemis*, which was somewhat typical of the rumrunner ships, was fifty-two feet long with three Liberty engines. The ship could do forty-five knots—which in landlubber terms is about fifty-one miles an hour. When ordered to stop by the Coast Guard, the *Artemis* sped up, hoping to outrun its pursuers. The patrol boat opened fire and shot more than one hundred rounds at the fleeing ship. At least thirty or forty struck the *Artemis* and two of her crew. John Johnson and Captain Carl Reiter, both of Greenport, were wounded in the onslaught of gunfire.

After enduring the barrage of bullets, the *Artemis* turned and rammed the Coast Guard cutter, crippling it on the port side, before escaping from the patrol and landed on the beach at Orient. Scrambling to get help for their wounded comrades, the crew woke up George Edwards and William Haberman of Orient to take Johnson and Reiter up to the hospital. According to reports, Johnson had been shot in the head, while Reiter had taken six bullets in his body.

As the injured men were taken to Eastern Long Island Hospital, the cargo on the *Artemis* was hastily unloaded. Some of the liquor was loaded into three dories, which were later caught. Investigators, realizing that some of the crew must have been hit in the hail of bullets, went to the hospital and made inquiries. A fast-thinking local doctor saved Johnson and Reiter from arrest, claiming that their wounds were from a hunting accident.[179]

The remaining crew moved the heavily damaged *Artemis* with the help of the fishing boat *Evangeline* quietly up the sound to Port Jefferson. Prohibition officials had set investigators to watch most of the boatyards along the sound for the ship. William Fillbach, a DA in Port Jefferson, spotted the ship at Long Island Shipyard in Port Jefferson Harbor.[180] Fillbach reported that the *Artemis* was a "scene of chaos. The cabin was strewn with glass. One handle of the wheel had been shot away, and nine machine gun bullet holes were counted in the windshield. Four of them were directly behind the wheel....Both sides of the *Artemis* had been riddled by bullets. Three planks on her port side for a distance of over six feet [above the waterline] had been stove in."[181]

Fillbach and five other deputy sheriffs guarded what remained of the boat, while authorities tried to figure out if they had the ability to confiscate the vessel. *Artemis* was in dry dock and did not have a drop of booze anywhere on board, although the scent of it lingered in the air.[182] Possession of the ship hung in limbo until mid-September, when U.S. Marshal Fred Pulver seized the vessel for nonpayment of a bill to Eastern Gafga Shipyard in Greenport.[183]

FRANK ZEWENSKEY'S FARM IN Cutchogue was raided one quiet December night in 1931. Agents suspected that the farm was a "drop" or holding area for liquor that was shipped in before it could be moved up the island and visited Zewenskey. After denying that there was any liquor on the premises, Zewenskey suggested that the officials search the property. Officers soon noticed the scent of alcohol in the barn. After searching both the main floor and the second floor of the structure, they were about to give up when Deputy Sheriff Bertram Walker discovered a secret door leading off a small room through a double partition into a hidden room. There they found a hoard of two hundred cases of three different brands of scotch packed into bags. Further investigation led to the discovery of a well-built staircase leading down the bluff to Long Island Sound. When confronted, Zewenskey confessed that a truck had broken down in front of his property the night before and the drivers had abandoned the load, but they were supposed to return the next night. He informed officials that he could get fifteen cents per bag for storage. Unable to find a truck to haul off their find, officials ended up hiring one of Zewensky's trucks to move the booze into the city.[184]

MONETARILY, THE MOST EXPENSIVE cargo seized in Southold was found in June 1931. The yacht *Surf*, a steam-powered beauty, was two hundred feet long and fitted as a rich man's pleasure craft, complete with a radio. The yacht, captained by James Hayes of Greenport with a crew of fifteen sailors, was caught by Lieutenant Elmer F. Stone of the Coast Guard destroyer *Cummings* off Montauk with four thousand cases of whiskey worth about $300,000. Including the yacht, which was seized, the estimated value of the capture was over $500,000. The captain was sentenced to three months in prison.[185]

TWO YOUNG MEN FROM Water Mill soon found out that the bootlegging business was very dangerous. The organized crime faction running the importation of alcohol on the East End was intent on keeping a tight control on the business and doing away with competitors. A bitter feud broke out between competing gangs working in Sag Harbor, East Hampton and Southampton. In June 1931, a group of young men late-night socializing in Southampton were forced into a car at one o'clock in the morning. Realizing that something was very wrong, Herbert Miller and Mack McGee managed to escape the car before it started down the road. William Kelly got away from the kidnappers when the car pulled into some woods. The

Once the largest whaling port on Long Island, Sag Harbor was deeply mired in the rumrunning and bootlegging trade during Prohibition. *Author's collection.*

two remaining youths, Thomas Farrell and Jacob Antilely, were dragged into an abandoned house in North Sea, and their kidnappers proceeded to beat and torture them by using a red-hot potato masher heated on an oil lamp to brand their faces, necks, hands and feet. The assailants accused the young men of hijacking a load of liquor from their gang several nights earlier. At dawn, the pair were dumped near Southampton. Henry Thiele, Charles Walker and Frank Alfred were charged with the crime. Joseph Stimson and Betty Mack, both of New Jersey, were held as possible accessories, since the accused were reputed to be staying in a house Stimson and Mack had rented. Walker was later acquitted. Later during the trial, through cross-examination, Thomas Farrell testified that a large Filipino man, who was never caught, was responsible for torturing him.[186]

THE RUMRUNNING BUSINESS WAS successful because of organized crime's use of technology. Wireless radios sent coded messages to place orders, arrange drop-offs and warn of possible capture by federal authorities. In Sag Harbor, Stephen O'Neill of Southampton was discovered along with a hoard of two hundred cases of scotch. In November 1931, authorities intercepted a coded message and began searching for the source. After triangulating the signal, officials eventually discovered the transmitter was in a bungalow near Peconic Bay in Sag Harbor. O'Neill was discovered by two Prohibition officers and two U.S. marshals who raided the building. Katherine Gray, who denied any knowledge of the operation, was discovered in bed on the second floor of the building and was also taken into custody. William Schultz was arrested when he drove up to the cottage while the raid was taking place.[187]

THE BRITISH SHIP *TEMISCOUDA* decided that rather than wait outside the territorial waters of the United States for the rumrunner boats, it would bring the cargo directly to shore. Unfortunately for the crew of six, the Coast Guard boat 288 spotted *Temiscouda* as it tried to slip into Fort Pond Bay in Montauk. Loaded with one hundred cases, the ship was fired on when it refused to stop. Luckily, when a bullet pierced the speeding ship's gasoline tank, the gas just leaked out instead of exploding. The crew surrendered to the boarding party and was eventually taken into custody by customs officials.[188]

IT WAS A SOLEMN day for some members of the Quogue Station Coast Guard. John Harlan and his men were on their way to Center Moriches, where they were going to meet up with a crew from the Forge River station and head to Bay Shore to provide an armed salute at a military funeral to bid farewell to a World War I soldier. Imagine Harlan's and his crew's surprise when they pulled up to the public dock in Center Moriches in their service dory to find a group of men transferring a load of liquor from a powerboat to several nearby trucks.

When confronted, the bootleggers scattered. One managed to hop into a partially laden truck and escape. Joe Tuttle of Eastport, a former Coast Guard member, was one of the three men aboard the boat unloading and leaped overboard in an effort to swim away from the arresting officials, but he was soon caught. In a bid to erase the evidence, William Powers, lit a match and set the boat on fire.

As the boat began to burn, the Forge River squad pulled up to the dock. The fire department was summoned, and twenty-one cases of liquor were salvaged from the remains of the boat. Instead of continuing on to the funeral, the Quogue Coast Guard squad elected to escort Tuttle, Powers and William Duffy (the third man) up to Brooklyn for arraignment.[189]

ATTORNEY GENERAL JOHN J. Bennett of Greene County, New York, had his attention focused on taking down the sprawling syndicate run by Jack Diamond. The syndicate was said to have tentacles across Long Island, New York City, Dutchess, Ulster and Albany. While Diamond's influence in Suffolk County appeared to be low, Bennett claimed to have found documents linking the famed gangster to the area via Vannie Higgins and Leo Steinberg.

Rumors of the situation linked Diamond's name to the beer and ale distribution. Gang associates had main distribution centers in both Port Jefferson and Riverhead. Raids on other sites run by Diamond's group turned up fake labels for popular beers from Canada, which were often available in Suffolk.[190]

WHILE NEWSPAPERS ENJOYED DEDICATING space to breathlessly reporting the capture of various bootleggers and rumrunners, rarely did they dedicate space to the closure of speakeasies found in the county. However, in early May, Prohibition officers headquartered in Bay Shore turned their attention to these illegal bars. Orin J. Meade, lead enforcer in Suffolk County, had his men raid the former Yaphank Grange while a dance was in progress. Under the fascinated gaze of the dancers, John Tankes and George Baker—partners and proprietors of the site—as well as former special constable John Bennett of Farmingdale, who was acting as the bartender, were all arrested when officials discovered twenty-eight cases of beer and bottles of whiskey on the premises. In the basement of the hall, agents found a distillery with vats of mash.[191]

Medford Community Hall had a bowling alley, stage, kitchen, restaurant and bar. German-born Ernest Herr was manager when it was raided. *From the* Mid-Island Mail, *April 6, 1938, page 1.*

That was not the only dance federal agents crashed that night. Later on, after breaking up the dance and distillery at Yaphank, agents traveled to Medford Community Hall and arrested Ernest Herr for possession and sale of liquor. The same group also visited the Bohemia hotel and arrested Cyril Chovanec. This was the second raid on Chovanec's hotel; the first raid, which happened over the end-of-year festivities, resulted in no charges against the proprietor.[192]

WHO KNEW THAT BEING a real estate agent in the Hamptons could be a chancy occupation? At least, that was probably running through E.T. Dayton's mind when he was showing a beach cottage to a prospective client in October 1931. Walter Keck's cottage, which was a short distance from the Georgica Coast Guard Station, was up for grabs. As Dayton was showing the place, he opened the garage to reveal one hundred kegs of liquor piled up. The discovery probably cut the tour short, but by the time officials arrived to take control of the booze, not a drop was found.[193]

1932

In May, during a raid on a barn in Cutchogue, investigators found one of the most elaborate shortwave radio sets they had ever discovered installed in an automobile. Edward Zuchoski, the owner of the barn, was arrested along with Patrick Fitzpatrick of the Bronx and Elmer Linton of Manhattan. Authorities stated they were sure that the radio was used to communicate with rumrunners. In a bonus for investigators in a nearby house, another radio was detected operating. When officials burst into the home, they discovered Anna Harris, a radio operator, and immediately arrested her, seizing not only her radio set but also 160 gallons of liquor.[194]

AROUND AND AROUND PLUM Island they went, the fifty-five-foot liquor boat in the front and the seventy-five-foot Coast Guard boat close behind. By its longest dimension, Plum Island is barely three miles long, and there are dangerous spots for navigation on all sides. Since it was night, neither boat could recklessly cut corners—the two boats went around the island like horses on the merry-go-round.

It all started when the rumrunner came sailing along. When it saw the Coast Guard boat, it turned and slid around Plum Island as if trying to avoid attention. The Coast Guard boat began to follow slowly at first and then faster as the rumrunner picked up speed. Round and round the island the two boats went.

Eventually, the rumrunner slowed down and permitted the Coast Guard on board to search the ship. There was no liquor aboard—there never had been. The rumrunner in question was only a decoy, behind it at a respectful distance had been another speedboat with eight hundred sacks of whiskey aboard. On the signal from the first boat, the second boat had swung south as the Plum Island chase began and sneaked in through Gardiners Bay. Finally, it landed its cargo of whiskey in Greenport while the Coast Guard was distracted.[195]

EARLY IN THE MORNING at the end of May 1932, the Coast Guard was surprised to find a ship, *Bali* of Bridgeport, Connecticut, and its crew aground on Fishers Island high on Chocomount Beach. After investigating, officials discovered in the ship (and the waters around it) 116 sacks of liquor. It took two patrol boats to secure the scene from the local residents and gather up all the sacks.[196]

THINGS WERE NOT GOING well at the Blue Point Coast Guard Station in January 1932. After a rumrunner had run aground near the station and was set on fire after its cargo was removed, suspicions that the station crew may have been in league with the rumrunners were investigated. Fire Island, Bellport and Georgica were also closely scrutinized. Coast Guard officials stated that four guardsmen were tried and found guilty of taking bribes and twenty others stood accused.

The shakeup moved half of all the guardsmen stationed on Long Island inland and brought newcomers from the Great Lakes to the shoreline. Figures such as Owney Madden and Vannie Higgins were named as being involved in the bribery.[197]

In an effort to break organized crime's smuggling ring, the federal government finally began to move against some of the men they felt were the backbone of the ring. Frank Russell of Parksley Virginia, a former Coast Guard man stationed at Blue Point, was charged with bribing Solomon Outlau, Joshua Austin, Manuel Lawrence and Earl Fulcher of Coast Guard Picket Boat 2328, which was stationed in Fire Island Inlet. Wolferd "Solly" Koman of West Sayville, who was a close friend of W. Clifford Wilson of Patchogue; Julian Schultze; and George Beckman of Bay Shore were charged with bribing Coast Guard members. Others also swept up in the same net were Edward Baker of Patchogue and Bay Shore and Harry Howard and Cecil Wessels of Napeague, John Rossa, Fred Stengal, Edward Baker, Charles Steinberg, as well as Steinberg's daughter Doris Green and her husband, Edward J. Green, all of whom were also convicted of bribery.[198]

HUNDREDS OF RESIDENTS OF Greenport and Orient watched fascinated as the Coast Guard chased a rum boat one night in May. While that boat got away, one with a large cargo was seized by Quogue. The next night, Charles Samuelson of College Point, the engineer on the sixty-foot speedboat *Scipio*, was wounded as the Coast Guard machinegunned the *Scipio*. Struck on the right side of his head, he suffered a fractured skull. His comrades—Captain Joseph Knowles of New Bedford, Massachusetts; Thomas A Stone of Fairfield, Connecticut; and John White of Bridgeport, Connecticut—were all arrested.

Thirty men gathered on the beach between the Tiana and Quogue Coast Guard Stations at the deepest part of the night. The men were there to unload two hundred cases of wine and assorted liquors. Suspicious of the activity on Rum Row, Harold L. Carter of the Quogue Station gathered eight men from both stations to do a sweep of the beach.

As the guards made their way through the night, they came across thirty men unloading a boat. Desperate to finish the job, one of the smugglers pulled a pistol and fired toward the Coast Guard crew. The bullet hit Leslie Randall, a surfman from the Tiana Coast Guard Station. Luckily for Randall, the bullet passed between his arm and grazed his left side. Startled by the shot, the smugglers fled into the night. Authorities managed to grab three of the men: Sol Rosenberg of New York City, Jack O'Keefe of Jamaica and Jack Sidney of Brooklyn.[199]

YOU NEVER KNOW WHAT type of people will rent your home while you are away, as Mr. and Mrs. Allen Doyle of Paradise Point in Southold discovered much to their dismay. Their home was raided by Department of Justice agents who discovered that tenants Patrick Fitzgerald and Elmer Linton had a shortwave radio that they had hastily dismantled as the agents were closing in on the residence.

For Fitzgerald and Linton, this was their second brush with the law; two weeks earlier, they had been arrested at Edward Zuchowsky's farm in Cutchogue with a shortwave radio set in their car. The pair had skipped out on their bail and set up another radio to continue their work in Southold.[200]

IN 1932, TOWN SUPERVISOR John Hoffman found himself in a sticky situation. The town of Southold had always been a mostly peaceful place. So peaceful that it had just one police officer for the whole 404-square-mile town, Special Officer Patrick Kelley. Unfortunately for Hoffman, Kelley had just been arrested when his father's farm was raided by Prohibition agents. When Kelley's property was searched, a secret trapdoor in the garage was found leading to a tunnel and a storage pit, which had fifty bags of rye. Kelley and his father, J.P., were swept up and charged with possession of intoxicating liquors and having an illegal radio station in the house. Both men were released on bail. Officer Kelley stated that he was not involved in any rumrunning, he simply boarded with his father. Hoffman quietly suspended Kelley from his job pending the judgment of the courts.[201] The verdict must have been favorable,

Despite being brought up on charges of violating the Volstead Act, Patrick Kelley had a long and distinguished career in the Southold Police Department. *Courtesy of the Southold Historical Museum, Southold, New York.*

because Kelley went on to have a long career in the Southold Police, which two years later expanded to an eight-man department.

Two rum running boats, heavily laden with holiday liquor were seized off Long Island last week by the Coast Guards. The fishing schooner Harold, *supposedly loaded with codfish, was found to contain 600 cases of booze hidden under about 12 tons of the marine creatures. It was because the schooner was riding so low in the water that the Coast Guards became suspicious. The* Harold *was taken off Montauk Point and at about the same time the speedboat* Colin *was captured at Jones Inlet with 150 cases aboard.*[202]

NEAR OX ISLAND IN the Great South Bay, Captain Steve Austin made his living as a bayman, fishing and catching eels. After setting his eel pots late one afternoon, he retired to bed on his boat. During the night, he awoke to the sound of a powerful engine nearby. The other vessel sounded like it was aground on a nearby sandbar. Not wanting trouble, Austin rolled over and soon fell back asleep. The next morning, he checked his eel pots, bringing in a small catch. Not seeing any other vessels nearby, he moved over to the sandbar where he thought he heard the other ship on during the night. There among the eelgrass was a rope; as Austin pulled on it, he found it was tied to a sack with whiskey. As Austin continue pulling on the rope, more and more bottles of different wines and whiskies appeared, a total eighteen cases of booze. Returning to shore, Austin sold his total catch, $20 in fish, and, to the local speakeasy, $900 of liquor.[203]

OTHER REMEMBRANCES

Not all of the liquor passing thorough East End came from overseas. The Hedges barn in East Marion was located on Bay Avenue. Henry Hedges and his sister Jessie ran a popular duck and chicken farm and had a stand on the side of the road. Their barn, where they incubated their chicks, had a number of gurgling pipes overhead. They let visitors know that the pipes were used to keep the incubators with the tiny chicks alive. However, the pipes actually served a dual purpose: they not only kept the barn warm for the incubators but also connected to the whiskey still in the back room.[204]

SOME SOUTHOLD RESIDENTS REMEMBER the members of organized crime who came to Southold to work in the rumrunning and bootlegging trade. On Hogs Neck, men such as Frank Costello, Dutch Schultz, Oney Madden and Two Fingered Genovese lived in Bayview. Even though they were well paid, farmers and residents in the area—whether or not they wanted to be involved in storing the contraband—were sometimes coerced with threats to cooperate. "They had this new-found money and they really didn't know how to use it and I guess, they, they recognized they might not have it long so they would do everything in excess, they would decide they wanted to take up golf and they would buy the most expensive golf clubs and after finding out it wasn't that easy, why they would bend them or break them."[205]

Another resident remembered

the big gray house that was the headquarters for the rumrunners. And they would light the thing up at nighttime with every light in the house put on, you know, and then these oyster boats that we were talking about, they would come along here and they'd go up to Cedar Beach Point and they'd like run aground out there and then all night long they'd be trucks going up and getting whiskey and stuff and bringing it down.... They were a rough bunch in there....Some of the guys were pretty nice, of course, I was a little kid then and I used to make friends with them, you know. And they all had guns and I'd, you know, I had a single shot one and if I could afford a pack of cartridges, you know, that was a lot for me. They would come over and let me have their gun and it was like an automatic...and they had a pulley post out there and we used to shoot that, you know. Finally, cut the thing right off, hit it so many times.[206]

OFTEN FAMILIES WHO LIVED along the shoreline were not given the opportunity to object to being drawn into the smuggling. Residents remember as children boxes of liquor appearing in their garages or sheds overnight to disappear within days. Usually, a couple of bottles were left behind in thanks by the visitors.[207]

In the mid-1920s, when Johnnie Piccozzi was fourteen, he began to work nights at Sage's brickyard, shoveling coal to keep the fires burning in the kilns. He kept the job all through his high school years. At the yard, a deep-water channel ran from the bay to the brickyard docks. Sage's shipped bricks up and down the coast in their own boats. One day, Johnnie and his friends were approached by rumrunners and offered $750 each per boat for unloading cases of liquor ashore. Sometimes there were two to three boats per night. This was unheard of wealth to a farm boy who made $3 a week for hours and hours of hard physical labor. What to do with so much money? They couldn't take it home, or their parents would raise the roof and ruin everything. So they hid their loot in tin cans and buried it until they needed it. Thus they kept their secret not only from their parents but also from the owners of the brickyard.[208]

SPARKY COYLE OF GREENPORT noted that even just everyday events could be fraught with danger. A friend of his was standing on the side of Route 25 just west of Greenport trying to hitch a ride up to New York City. Suddenly, a truck pulled over in front of him, and the driver leaned out of the window, slapped a wad of something into his hand and accelerated away. Bemused, the man looked at what the driver had put into his hand and discovered he held a veritable fortune, fifty dollars in singles! He realized that where he was standing trying to catch a ride was actually the payoff point of one of the gangs of rumrunners. The man decided that continuing to stand on the side of the road or even trying to head up to the city was not in his best interests, so he skedaddled as fast as he could away from the roadway.[209]

OCCASIONALLY, EVIDENCE OF RUMRUNNING popped up years after Prohibition ended. Rumors abounded locally that the Naugles family was involved in the rumrunning business. It was whispered that when their barn burned down in 1936, the family, in the middle of the Great Depression, was able to quickly come up with cash to rebuild a handsome new barn. Years later, the Naugles house and barn were abandoned when the land was sold to a corporation. When the home was being renovated, in one of the upstairs bedrooms workers removed a false wall in a closet and discovered stacks and stacks of gin labels. Confirming the rumors that had been whispered more than seventy years earlier, today the handsome Naugles barn built with rumrunning money can still be seen at Hallockville Museum Farm.[210]

AS THE 1920S ROLLED into the 1930s, many of the professional rumrunners and bootleggers decided that landing shipments so far east and then moving the product up to New York City was unprofitable. Alcohol was increasingly transported farther west, with more landings happening in and around New York City. Popular landing areas dotted the shoreline in and around New York Harbor and the coastal areas of New Jersey and Delaware.

By early 1933, the Grand Experiment, Prohibition, was over for a nation that was exhausted by the battles waged between the government and forces of organized crime. And adults everywhere raised their glasses in a heartfelt toast that could be legally savored again.

CODE BOOK

Samuel W. Boerum, a fisherman, was plying his trade out in the waters of Peconic Bay near Greenport. Boerum, who mostly fished in Gardiner's Bay and Peconic Bay, was working on his boat the *Aglia* when a rumrunner raced past closely followed by a Coast Guard boat in hot pursuit. A small object flew out of the lead boat and plopped into the net Boerum was starting to haul up from the water.

Among the fish caught in the net was a small brown notebook. Curious, Boerum plucked it out of the net and soon realized what he had in his hands, an incredibly valuable and dangerous object. Valuable because the object was a notebook with a neatly typed list of all the codes that the local rumrunners used to communicate with one another. Dangerous because if anyone knew he had it or if he turned it in to authorities and word got out—it could be a death sentence for him and his family at the hands of powerful gangs who dodged the U.S. Coast Guard daily.

A stanch Methodist family, the Boerums did not drink, so Prohibition wasn't a hardship. Although the family supported a temperance lifestyle, Boerum did not want to be caught in dangerous situation. Whether he was mindful of the value to history the notebook represented or more probably worried that a rumrunner was going to knock on his door and demand the notebook back, Boerum did not destroy the little book. Rather he carefully dried it out and put the book away.

Eventually, the book was passed to his grandson Donald H. Boerum, a passionate local historian. Recognizing the value of the notebook as a symbol of the Prohibition era in Southold Town, he donated the book to the archives of the Oysterponds Historical Society.

The notebook shows that the smuggling ring had landing sites that stretched from Cape Hatteras to Orchard Beach, Maine. But the majority of its sites were concentrated from Long Island to Delaware.

Ambrose[211]	A17
Atlantic Highland Mandaley Pier[212]	A18
Ambrose Channel[213]	A19
Are you clear	A20
Are you on position yet	A21
Are you safe	A22
Alloway Creek[214]	A23
Arsonel warf at Pensgrove [sic][215]	A304
Are you sure of our position	A358
Also	A359
A piece	A360
And fifty	A361
And twenty-five	A362
And seventy-five	A363
After boat has loaded and left, wire me in what she has taken	A489
After boats are loaded and they all left, wire me what each one has taken	A490
At	A493
After you load	A494
And wait for second one	A508
And wait for the rest of them	A509
Are you sure	A510
Are you flashing your lights on proper time and proper way	A511

And wait for orders	A580
Ask	A581
And	A582
Are boats ready to leave	A583
Absecon or Atlantic City[216]	A625
Arrived	A777
Barnagat [sic][217]	B24
Belford[218]	B25
Bergen Point[219]	B26
Be prepared to go to any position when I give you final orders next schedule	B27
Boats	B28
Boat	B29
Be ready to work for	B30
Blinker flashing white west from ship John on Delaware side of channel	B31
Back creek	B32
Blinker flashing white East from ship John on Jersey side of channel	B33
Be ready to work tonight at	B513
Boats are here	B364
Boats not here yet	B365
Boats have not arrived	B366
Brands	
Gin	B367
Pints Rye	B368
Quarts Rye	B369
Standard Scotch	B370
Second Grade Scotch	B371

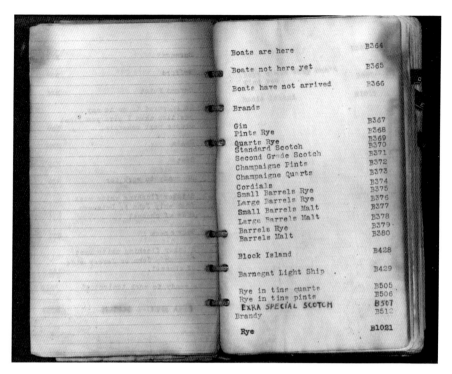

Boats are here · B364
Boats not here yet · B365
Boats have not arrived · B366

Brands

Gin · B367
Pints Rye · B368
Quarts Rye · B369
Standard Scotch · B370
Second Grade Scotch · B371
Champaigne Pints · B372
Champaigne Quarts · B373
Cordials · B374
Small Barrels Rye · B375
Large Barrels Rye · B376
Small Barrels Malt · B377
Large Barrels Malt · B378
Barrels Rye · B379
Barrels Malt · B380

Block Island · B428

Barnegat Light Ship · B429

Rye in tins quarts · B505
Rye in tins pints · B506
EXRA SPECIAL SCOTCH · B507
Brandy · B512

Rye · B1021

Apparently, gin, rye, scotch, champagne, cordials and malt are the standard inventory brought in by this particular rumrunning gang. *Courtesy of the Oysterponds Historical Society, Orient, New York.*

Champagne Pints	B372
Champagne Quarts	B373
Cordials	B374
Small Barrels Rye	B375
Large Barrels Rye	B376
Small Barrels Malt	B377
Large Barrels Malt	B378
Barrels Rye	B379
Barrels Malt	B380
Block Island[220]	B428
Barnegat Light Ship[221]	B429

Tye in thins quarts [*sic*]	B505
Tye in Tins Pints [*sic*]	B506
Exra Special Scotch [*sic*]	B507
Brandy	B512
Rye	B1021
By	B584
Boys claim they can't find you	B585
Bodie Island[222]	B1017
Coal Docks	C34
Cliffwood[223]	C35
Chalk Works[224]	C36
Come in tonight	C37
Change your call to	C38
Cutter—4 Stacker	C39
Cutter—3 Stacker	C40
Cutter—125 footer	C41
Cutter—100 footer	C42
Cutter—75 footer	C43
Cutter—White	C44
Compass Points	
North	C45
Nrtheast [*sic*]	C46
East	C47
Southeast	C48
South	C49
Southwest	C50
West	C51

Northwest	C52
Cataret ferry [sic][225]	C53
Cohansey River [sic][226]	C54
Cape Henlopen point[227]	C55
Cape May Point[228]	C56
Can't say now will let you know next schedule	C57
Can you make it by	C58
Come in tonight to —	C59
Can't say now. Delayed by bad weather	C305
Can not give you accurate time till I get bearing	C306
Count what they take	C381
Cannot be there until	C382
Come up the middle	C383
Can you bring her to	C384
Can you bring her in?	C385
Can the Old Man bring her to	C386
Cape Cod[229]	C430
Come back	C514
Continue flashing	C563
Come in with boat that takes your last load	C564
Can you see flash of	C586
Can he see flash of	C587
Custom boat is in the	C588
$1/4$	C626
$1/2$	C627
$3/4$	C628
Can you see	C629

Can he see	C630
Cruiser type	C631
Coming in	C632
Carry out original orders	C778
Cancel last message	C779
Coney Island Creek[230]	C1011
Chesapeake Light Ship[231]	C1013
Cape Charles[232]	C1014
Cape Henry[233]	C1015
Currituck Beach Light[234]	C1016
Cape Hatteras[235]	C1018
Come in To	C1020
North	C649
North ¼ East	C650
North ½ East	C651
North ¾ East	C652
North by East	C653
North by East ¼ East	C654
North by East ½ East	C655
North by East ¾ East	C656
North North East	C657
North East by North ¾ North	C658
North East by North ½ North	C659
North East by North ¼ North	C660
North East by North	C661
North East ¾ North	C662
North East ½ North	C663

North East ¼ North	C664
North East	C665
North East ¼ East	C666
North East ½ East	C667
North East ¾ East	C668
North East by East	C669
North East by East ¼ East	C670
North East by East ½ East	C671
North East by East ¾ East	C672
North West by West ¾ West	C673
North West by West ½ West	C674
North West by West ¼ West	C675
North West by West	C676
North West ¾ West	C677
North West ½ West	C678
North West ¼ West	C679
North West	C680
North West ¼ North	C681
North West ½ North	C682
North West ¾ North	C683
North West by North	C684
North West by North ¼ North	C685
North West by North ½ North	C686
North West by North ¾ North	C687
North North West	C688
North By West ¾ West	C689
North by West ½ West	C690

North by West ¼ West	C691
North by West	C692
North ¾ West	C693
North ½ West	C694
North ¼ West	C695
East	C696
East ¼ South	C697
East ½ South	C698
East ¾ South	C699
East by South	C700
East by South ¼ South	C701
East by South ½ South	C702
East by South ¾ South	C703
East South East	C704
East North East	C705
East by North ¾ North	C706
East by North ½ North	C707
East by North ¼ North	C708
East by North	C709
East ¾ North	C710
East ½ North	C711
East ¼ North	C712
South	C713
South ¼ West	C714
South ½ West	C715
South ¾ West	C716
South by West	C717

South by West ¼ West	C718
South by West ½ West	C719
South by West ¾ West	C720
South South West	C721
South West by South ¾ South	C722
South West by South ½ South	C723
South West by South ¼ South	C724
South West by South	C725
South West ¾ South	C726
South West ½ South	C727
South West ¼ South	C728
South West	C729
South West ¼ West	C730
South West ½ West	C731
South West ¾ West	C732
South West by West	C733
South West by West ¼ West	C734
South West by West ½ West	C735
South West by West ¾ West	C736
South East by East ¾ East	C737
South East by East ½ East	C738
South East by East ¼ East	C739
South East by East	C740
South East ¾ East	C741
South East ½ East	C742
South East ¼ East	C743
South East	C744

South East ¼ South	C745
South East ½ South	C746
South East ¾ South	C747
South East by South	C748
South East by South ¼ South	C749
South East by South ½ South	C750
South East by South ¾ South	C751
South East by South ¾ South	C751
South South East	C752
South by East ¾ East	C753
South by East ½ East	C754
South by East ¼ East	C755
South by East	C756
South ¾ East	C757
South ½ East	C758
South ¼ East	C759
West	C760
West ¼ North	C761
West ½ North	C762
West ¾ North	C763
West by North	C764
West by North ¼ North	C765
West by North ½ North	C766
West by North ¾ North	C767
West North West	C768
West South West	C769
West by South ¾ South	C770

West by South ½ South	C771
West by South ¼ South	C772
West by South	C773
West ¾ South	C774
West ½ South	C775
West ¼ South	C776
Dental works	D60
Don't come in to-night	D61
Days	
Sunday	D62
Monday	D63

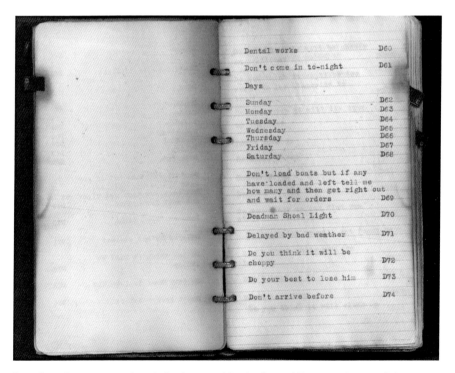

Page from the rumrunner's code book rescued by the Samuel Boerum. *Courtesy of the Oysterponds Historical Society, Orient, New York.*

140

Tuesday	D64
Wednesday	D65
Thursday	D66
Friday	D67
Saturday	D68
Don't load boat but if any have loaded and left tell me how many and then get right out and wait for orders	D69
Deadman Shoal Light[236]	D70
Delayed by bad weather	D71
Do you think it will be choppy	D72
Do your best to lose him	D73
Don't arrive before	D74
Do you think it will be choppy on position?	D307
Do you think it would be too rough to lay alongside to load?	D308
Do you think it will die down by tonight?	D309
Don't come to	D310
Delaware River[237]	D311
Dennis Creek[238]	D312
Degrees	D349
Do you think we can find you at	D387
Do you think it will get foggy	D495
Don't flash while you are loading	D515
Don't load	D556
Don't load him	D557
Do you think it will clear up	D565
Don't come in unless your boat is all unloaded	D589
Diamond Shoals Light Ship[239]	D1019

141

Eight	E75
Eight miles E.S.E. from five fathom lightship	E76
Egg Island Point[240]	E77
Ease in	E78
Easing in	E388
Fort Hamilton[241]	F79
Fort Wadsworth[242]	F80
Fryes Dock[243]	F81
Further instructions tomorrow	F82
Further instructions later	F83
Four	F84
Five	F85
Forty miles E.S.E. from five fathom lightship	F86
Five fathom lightship[244]	F87
Further instructions next schedule	F313
Ferry wharf at Pensgrove [sic][245]	F314
For wind	F315
For weather	F316
Fifty	F389
Fire Island Light Ship[246]	F431
Fenwick Shoal Light Ship[247]	F432
Flash while you are loading, but make sure that no cutters are around	F516
Fisherman type	F533
From	F558
For how many more days have you got oil before you have to start to go back	F590
Fire Island Inlet[248]	F1007

Great Beds Red[249]	G88
Go to Saint Pierre[250]	G89
Go to Liverpool N.S.[251]	G90
Go to Halifax[252]	G91
Go to Lunenburg[253]	G92
Get out and wait for orders	G93
Go to Scotland position anywhere off shore that you are safe judging weather	G94
Give this message to man in charge of small boats	G95
Go to	G317
Give him	G433
Go to any position of Block Island you are safe judging weather	G434
Go to any position of Nantucket Light Ship you are safe judging weather	G435
Go to any position of Cape Code you are safe judging weather	G436
Go to any position of Fire Island Light Ship you are safe judging weather	G437
Go to any position of Fenwick Light Ship you are safe judging weather	G438
Go to any position of Winter Quarter Shoal Light Ship you are safe judging weather	G439
Give man in charge of boat slip with amount he has taken	G440
Give him more if he can take it	G517
Give me your present position	G518
Get some oil from	G591
Give me an account of what you have left on board	G592
Give	G593
Give me number of boat that is there	G594
Go to any position off Absecon or Atlantic City you are safe judging weather	G633

Highlands[254]	H96
Harrison[255]	H97
Have loaded	H98
How many got there	H99
Has arrived	H100
Has left	H101
How many have loaded	H102
How is the weather? Do you think we can work tonight	H103
Have the boats left yet?	H104
How is the weather? Can we load small boats tonight?	H105
How is the weather for coming all the way in tonight?	H106
Has —— arrived	H107
How does it look to you?	H108
How soon can you make it?	H109
How hard is it blowing?	H318
Hundred	H390
Have patience	H422
He will be there	H496
Halifax, N.S.[256]	H595
How long can you wait on your present position before you must get on the way to be at	H596
Hog Island Light[257]	H1012
I am picketed	I-110
I have sent out	I-111
I can make it	I-112
I cannot make it	I-113
Inside	I-114

Is answer yes or no?	I-115
I am safe	I-116
Is everything O.K?	I-117
I will arrive at ——	I-118
I can be there sooner if you wish	I-119
I will be late	I-120
Instead of	I-319
Is it foggy outside?	I-320
Is it misty?	I-321
It is misty	I-322
Is there a big sea rolling?	I-323
Is it blowing hard off shore?	I-324
If you want us I can make it	I-391
In case of emergency	I-423
Is coming out	I-441
Is it foggy or clear?	I-497
Is not coming out	I-519
It is choppy	I-520
It is foggy	I-521
It is very rough	I-522
I am sending	I-597
Is	I-598
Is here cannot see flash of	I-599
I am on position and flashing light as per orders	I-601
I was chased	I-645
I am being chased	I-646
If you get unloaded don't come in	I-647

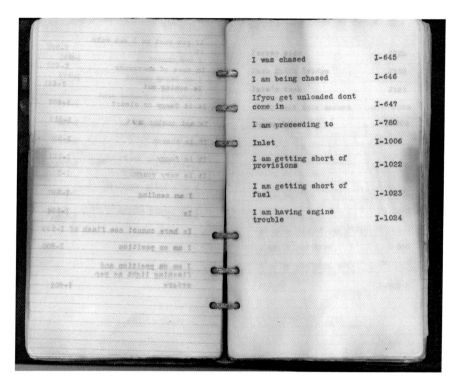

A code for just about every eventuality appears in the book found in Greenport. *Courtesy of the Oysterponds Historical Society, Orient, New York.*

I am proceeding to	I-780
Inlet	I-1006
I am getting short of provisions	I-1022
I am getting short of fuel	I-1023
I am having engine trouble	I-1024
Jersey side	J121
Jack Knife Bridge[258]	J122
Jake's dock[259]	J123
Just load this amount	J392
Jones Inlet[260]	J1008
Kasbay Brick Yard[261]	K124

Keansburg[262]	K125
Keyport[263]	K126
Keyport Buoy, flashing white	K127
Keep stern light on for five minutes every fifteen minutes	K128
Keep stern light out	K129
Keep coming	K130
Keep dim light on visible all around from appointed time on until boats arrive	K350
Look for single light if you see boat all lit up. Keep clear	L131
Look for skiff	L132
Look for Light on the shed	L133
Latitude	L325
Longitude	L326
Load them as fast as possible	L393
Load	L394
Load him just the same	L395
Load all of them	L396
Liverpool, N.S.[264]	L602
Liberty job is in the	L603
Monument #1 Flashing White[265]	M134
Monument #2 Flashing Green[266]	M135
Monument #3 Flashing White[267]	M136
Monument #4 Flashing Red[268]	M137
Monument #5 Flashing White[269]	M138
Morgan[270]	M139
Main Channel	M140
Miles	M141

Mill Creek[271]	M142
Mad Horse[272]	M143
Make sure	M144
Make reply as short as possible	M145
Make it	M327
Moon	M351
Make arrangements if you have to put it back. Let him wait for you until	M424
Make sure you count what he takes	M442
Montauk Point[273]	M443
Make arrangements	M559
Mixed	M604
New York side	N146
Narrows	N147
Nine	N148
Numbers	
1	N149
2	N150
3	N151
4	N152
5	N153
6	N154
7	N155
8	N156
9	N157
0	N158
No	N159
No wind here	N160

Notify me a day before you want me	N161
10	N328
20	N329
30	N330
40	N331
50	N332
60	N333
70	N334
80	N335
90	N336
100	N337
Number	N352
200	N397
300	N398
400	N399
500	N400
600	N401
700	N402
800	N403
900	N404
1000	N405
No good	N425
Nantucket Shoal Light Ship[274]	N444
Northeast End Light Ship[275]	N445
5	N566
15	N567
25	N568

35	N569
45	N570
55	N571
65	N572
75	N573
85	N574
95	N575
105	N576
Not to	N605
Occ. No 6 Red Gong[276]	O-162
Occ. No. 12 Red[277]	O-163
Occ. No. 15 Green[278]	O164
Occ. No. 18 Red Gong[279]	O-165
Occ. No. 26 Red Bell[280]	O-166
Old Orchard[281]	O-167
One	O-168
Outside	O-169
O.K.	O-426
Overfalls Light Ship[282]	O-446
Off	O-606
Only	O-781
Penn R.R. Bridge[283]	P170
Port Newark[284]	P171
Position #1 is 2 miles from point of Hook	P172
Ten miles S.E. from Scotland	P173
Ten miles S.S.E. from Scotland	P174
Put your lights on	P175

Put your lights out	P176
Picket has left us	P177
One mile and one-half N.W. from Shrewsbury Rock light[285]	P178
Six miles S.E. from Scotland	P179
Five miles S.E. from Scotland	P180
Northeast by east from Ambrose depth of water 31 feet	P181
North north east from Ambrose depth of water 30 feet	P182
Four miles S.E. from Scotland	P183
15 miles S.S.E. from Absecon or Atlantic City	P184
18 Miles E ¼ S from Absecon or Atlantic City	P185
8 miles southeast from Ambrose	P186
2 miles northwest from Fire Island Inlet blinker	P187
1 mile east of West End	P188
1 mile east of the north end of Asbury Park[286]	P189
¼ mile off Sea Breeze dock[287]	P190
Proceed to Delaware position anywhere off shore that you are safe judging weather	P191
¼ mile off the wreck	P192
15 miles S.E. from Scotland	P338
12 miles S.E. from Sea Girt light[288]	P339
Position	P340
5 miles S.E. from Sea Girt light	P341
Five miles S.E. from Ambrose lightship	P353
One mile due East from Red Electric Sign of Asbury Park	P355
Ten miles S.E. from Ambrose lightship	P356
Twenty miles S.E. from Ambrose lightship	P357
Put your light up on mast visible all around when you get on position for five minutes every fifteen minutes until boats arrive then put it out	P406

Pass word	P407
Ten miles due East of Sea Girt light	P408
Twelve miles due East of Sea Girt light	P409
Fifteen miles due East of Sea Girt light	P410
Fifteen miles S.E. from Ambrose lightship	P411
Ten miles E.S.E. from five fathom lightship	P412
Twelve mile E.S.E. from five fathom lightship	P413
Five miles E.S.E. from five Fathom lightship	P414
Fifteen miles E.S.E. from five fathom lightship	P415
Five miles due East of Cape Cod Highland Light[289]	P447
Eight miles due East of Cape Cod Highland light	P448
Twelve miles due East of Cape Cod Highland Light	P449
Twenty miles South by East from Sankaty Head Light[290]	P450
Five miles North North East from Nantucket Shoal Light Ship	P451
Ten mile North North East from Nantucket Shoal Light Ship	P452
Fifteen miles South by West from Gay Head Light[291]	P453
Twenty miles South by West from Gay Head Light	P454
Five miles South by East from Block Island South East light	P455
Eight miles South by East from Block Island South East Light	P56
Twelve miles South Bu East from Block Island South East Light	P457
Fifteen miles South by East from Block Island South East Light	P458
Five miles South from Montauk Point Light[292]	P459
Twelve miles South from Montauk Point Light	P460
Fifteen miles South from Montauk Point Light	P461
Five miles South from Shinnecock Light	P462
Twelve miles South from Shinnecock Light	P463
Fifteen miles South from Shinnecock Light	P464

Five miles South from Fire Island Light Ship	P465
Eight miles South from Fire Island Light Ship	P466
Ten miles South from Fire Island Light Ship	P467
Nine miles S.W. from Fire Island Light Ship	P468
Five miles South East from Barnegat Light Ship	P469
Eight miles South East from Barnegat Light Ship	P470
Ten miles South East from Barnegat Light Ship	P471
Three miles South East from Northeast End Light Ship	P472
Five miles South East from Northeast end Light Ship	P473
Eight miles South East from Northeast End light Ship	P474
Ten miles South East from Northeast End Light Ship	P475
Three miles South East from Fenwick Shoal Light Ship	P476
Five miles South East from Fenwick Shoal Light Ship	P477
Eight miles south East from Fenwick Shoal Light Ship	P478
Ten miles South East from Fenwick Shoal Light Ship	P479
Twelve miles South East from Overfalls Light Ship	P480
Three miles South East from Winter Quarter Shoal Light Ship	P481
Five miles South East from Winter Quarter Shoal Light Ship	P482
Eight miles South East from Winter Quarter Shoal Light Ship	P483
Ten miles South East from Winter Quarter Shoal Light Ship	P484
Five miles South East from Five Fathom Light Ship	P485
Ten miles South East from Five Fathom Light Ship	P486
Fifteen miles South East from Five Fathom Light Ship	P487
Twelve miles S.E. from Ambrose Light Ship	P491
Twelve miles S.E. from Scotland Light Ship	P492
15 miles south west from Fire Island Light Ship	P523
22 miles South West from Fire Island Light Ship	P524

10 miles East by South from Fire Island Light Ship	P525
15 Miles East by South from Fire Island Light Ship	P526
20 miles East by South from Fire Island Light Ship	P527
7 miles South East from Fire Island Light Ship	P528
10 miles South East from Fire Island Light Ship	P529
20 Miles South East from Scotland Light Ship	P534
20 Miles South East by South from Scotland Light Ship	P535
15 Miles South East by South from Scotland Light Ship	P536
15 Miles south East by East from Scotland Light Ship	P537
20 miles South East by East from Scotland Light Ship	P538
15 miles South East by East from Ambrose Light Ship	P539
20 miles South East by East from Ambrose Light Ship	P540
15 miles South East by South from Ambrose Light Ship	P541
20 miles South East by South from Ambrose Light Ship	P542
15 miles South East from Fire Island Light Ship	P543
15 miles South West from Fire Island Light Ship	P544
20 miles due South from Shinnecock Light	P545
Put up light on top of mast visible all around from appointed time until boats arrive and then put it out	P546
20 miles due East from Sea Girt Light	P547
25 miles South East from Shinnecock Light	P548
20 miles due South from Montauk Point Light	P549
20 mile South South East from Ambrose Light Ship[293]	P560
40 miles South East by South from Scotland Light Ship[294]	P578
40 miles South South East from Ambrose Light Ship	P579
50 miles South East by South from Scotland Light Ship	P607
50 miles South East by South from Ambrose Light Ship	P608

50 mile South South East from Scotland Light Ship	P609
40 miles South South East from Scotland Light Ship	P610
25 miles South South East from Scotland Light Ship	P611
20 Miles South South East from Scotland Light Ship	P612
20 miles South East from Absecon or Atlantic City Light	P634
25 mile South East from Absecon or Atlantic City Light	P635
25 mile South South East from Absecon or Atlantic City Light	P636
25 mile East by South from Absecon or Atlantic City Light	P637
25 mile South South West from Montauk Point	P638
10 miles due East from Northeast End light Ship	P639
40 miles due South from Montauk Point	P640
40 miles South South West from Montauk Point	P641
25 miles South East by South from Ambrose	P782
Romer Shoals[295]	R193
R.R. Bridge	R194
Robbins Reef[296]	R195
Raritan Bay[297]	R342
Rockaway Inlet[298]	R1010
Sea Girt[299]	S196
Scotland[300]	S197
Shrewsbury Rock[301]	S198
Sandy Hook[302]	S199
Sandy Hook Point[303]	S200
South River Brick Yard[304]	S201
South Channel[305]	S202
Stand by on radio steady until further orders	S203
Six	S204

Seven	S205
Six miles north west from Barnegat Light Ship	S206
South Amboy Coal Dock[306]	S207
Seawaren Dock [*sic*][307]	S208
Sea Breeze Point[308]	S209
Stow Creek[309]	S210
Schedule for outside	S211
6:30 a.m.	10:30 a.m.
4:00 p.m.	11:00 p.m.
Schedule for inside	S212
10:30 a.m.	4:00 p.m.
Eastern Standard Time	
Ship John light[310]	S213
Shall I be ready for ——	S214
Salem Creek[311]	S343
Stormy passage no sight. Not sure of position	S344
Stay on position until	S416
Seventy-Five	S417
Stay right on same position and wait for	S498
Shinnecock Light[312]	S530
Sloop type	S550
St. Pierre Miq [*sic*][313]	S613
Some oil	S614
Send him to	S615
Shark River[314]	S616
Skiff Type	S642

Stay on	S643
Turn around and get out	T215
Time	
1 a.m.	T216
2	T217
3	T218
4	T219
5	T220
6	T221
7	T222
8	T223
9	T224
10	T225
11	T226
12 noon	T227
13 (one p.m.)	T228
14 (two p.m.)	T229
15 (three p.m.)	T230
16 (four p.m.)	T231
17 (five p.m.)	T232
18 (six p.m.)	T233
19 (seven p.m.)	T234
20 (eight p.m.)	T235
21 (nine p.m.)	T236
22 (ten p.m.)	T237
23 (eleven p.m.)	T238
24 (midnight)	T239

Two	T240
Three	T241
Ten	T242
Time	
12:30 (a.m.)	T243
1:30	T244
2:30	T245
3:30	T246
4:30	T247
5:30	T248
6:30	T249
7:30	T250
8:30	T251
9:30	T252
10:30	T253
11:30	T254
12:30 (p.m.)	T255
1:30	T256
2:30	T257
3:30	T258
4:30	T259
5:30	T260
6:30	T261
7:30	T262
8:30	T263
9:30	T264
10:30	T265

11:30	T266
To miles east from Seagirt	T267
Ten miles S.E. from Seagirt	T268
Tonight	T269
Too risky	T270
Take no chances	T271
Take care you don't get picketed	T272
Tomorrow	T273
Too foggy	T345
Too much moon out	T354
Tell boys if they can't get in to come back to you	T418
Tonight at	T419
Twenty-five	T420
They will be there	T499
That is to meet you	T551
To make transfer	T561
To meet	T562
That is to meet you	T577
Tell him	T617
Tell them	T618
To be very careful	T619
Try and give him what he asks for	T620
To take	T621
To	T622
To wait for orders	T623
Until	U500
Wind	W274

Woodbridge Creek[315]	W275
When may we expect you on position?	W276
Wait for us on Jersey side of light	W277
Wait for us on New York side of light	W278
What is your position?	W279
Weather favorable	W280
Weather not favorable	W281
Weather too calm or smooth	W282
Weather may be better later	W283
Weather inside not suitable to work	W284
Will you be on time?	W285
What shall I do now?	W286
We can work tonight	W287
West bank	W288
When you get out wait for orders	W289
When you arrive there wire me	W290
Will meet you	W291
Will wait for you	W292
When can you be there?	W293
Whistle Buoy No. 2[316]	W294
Whistle Buoy No. 4[317]	W295
Whistle Buoy No.6[318]	W296
When boats get there call me. Tell me how many got there.	W297
When boats are loaded and leaving call me and tell me how may loaded.	W298
When did first one leave?	W299
When did last boat leave?	W300
Will wait for you in red sector of light	W301

Will wait for you in white sector of light	W302
What are the possibilities?	W346
What is the weather forecast for tonight?	W347
What direction is wind blowing from?	W348
What time can you make it	W421
What time?	W427
Winter Quarter Shoal Light Ship[319]	W488
Will they be able to find you	W501
What is the visability [sic]	W502
Wait for them	W503
Wait for him	W504
Wire me as soon as boat or boats get there	W531
Went back home light	W624
When it gets dark	W644
When you get on position put up two lights one above the other for five minutes every fifteen minutes until boats arrive and then put them out	W648
When you get clear	W783
Wire me as soon as boat or boats leave, what time she left and when they are all gone tell me what each one loaded	W532
When you get on position put all your running lights on and flash a light from the top of your mast visible all around for five minutes every fifteen minutes until boats arrive then put all your lights out	W552
When you get on position put all your running lights on for ten minutes and put them out for two minutes from appointed time until boats arrive and then put them out	W553
When you get on position put two lights one above the other on top of mast visible all around from appointed time until boats arrive and then put them out	W554
Yes	Y303

You get there on time	Y555
Zachs Inlet[320]	Z1009

If we can't communicate go to this position and stay there until someone comes to you

Lat. 3830 North
Long. 73 West

That puts you 73 miles E.S.E. from Five Fathom Light Ship

Special orders:
When I wire you saying will call you tonight, then you must wait for a call at twelve midnight, Eastern Standard Time and stay in for one-half hour.

The day you are coming in, you must stay on from 4:30 p.m. until you get in.

NOTES

Introduction

1. Metropolitan Museum of Art, Egyptian Old Dynasty 5, Bakers and Brewers c. 2446 to 2389 BC; EG592.
2. Carson, *Old Country Store*, 13–14.
3. Folk, "General Store on Long Island."
4. Clark, *Deliver Us from Evil*, 8, 14–20.
5. These figures were rough approximations because records racking the amounts being produced and consumed in the United States were not kept until the Civil War. The figures were calculated using the research conducted by the Temperance League in its campaign; Clark, *Deliver Us from Evil*, 14–20. While seven gallons over the course of a year doesn't sound like a large amount, in the 1970s, the average adult consumed only approximately two and a half gallons per year. Larkin, *Reshaping of Everyday Life*, 296.
6. Clark, *Deliver Us from Evil*, 39; Okrent, *Last Call*, 85.
7. Singer, *Prohibition on the Gold Coast*, 4.
8. Ibid.
9. *The Drunkard's Progress*, Currier and Ives Exhibit, Suffolk County Historical Society, Riverhead, New York, 2013.
10. Ledger book of the Oysterponds and Sterling Temperance Society held in the collection of the Oysterponds Historical Society, Orient, Suffolk County, New York.

11. Singer, *Prohibition on the Gold Coast*, 4.
12. Willoughby, *Rum War at Sea*, 9. In an interesting side note, many historians feel that the temperance movement was what gave women the practice, motivation and skills to form the suffrage movement.

Prohibition

13. NicKenzie Lawson, *Smugglers, Bootleggers, and Scofflaws*, 1.
14. Okrent, *Last Call*, 193; Clark, *Deliver Us from Evil*, 158–59; Singer, *Prohibition on the Gold Coast*, 92.
15. Okrent, *Last Call*, 144.
16. NicKenzie Lawson, *Smugglers, Bootleggers, and Scofflaws*, 59; Willoughby, *Rum War at Sea*, 14.
17. NicKenzie Lawson, *Smugglers, Bootleggers, and Scofflaws*, 60.
18. Ibid., 59–69; Okrent, *Last Call*, 170.
19. NicKenzie Lawson, *Smugglers, Bootleggers, and Scofflaws*, 72–73.
20. Merritt, "New York's Rum Row." Schultz was murdered in 1935 for disobeying the Commission (run by Siegel), which was the governing body of the American Mafia. Nickenzie Lawson, *Smugglers, Bootleggers, and Scofflaws*, 63.
21. NicKenzie Lawson, *Smugglers, Bootleggers, and Scofflaws*, 59–69. The Italian Mafia existed prior to Prohibition but only did business in the Italian ghettos of the city. "Lucky" Luciano and an associate named Doto started a side business—Murder, Incorporated—which got rid of inconvenient people.

How Did the Rumrunning Business Work?

22. Willoughby, *Rum War at Sea*, 17–18.
23. NicKenzie Lawson, *Smugglers, Bootleggers, and Scofflaws*, 1.
24. Ibid.
25. Ibid., 9; "Find Rum Hoard and Wireless," *Suffolk County News*, December 18, 1931.
26. Willoughby, *Rum War at Sea*, 105.
27. "$1,000 Bribery Trap Sprung in Suffolk," *New York Times*, May 1, 1932; "3 Nabbed in Cutchogue Booze Raid," *County Review*, May 5, 1932; "Find Rum Hoard and Wireless."

28. Mowry, "Listening to the Rumrunners," 6.
29. Ibid., 17.
30. NicKenzie Lawson, *Smugglers, Bootleggers, and Scofflaws*, 3; Okrent, *Last Call*, 278.
31. "Men Were Branded with Hot Irons in Hijacking Feud, They Say," *Patchogue Advance*, June 30, 1931; "Man and Woman Are Arrested in Bootleg Torture Case," *Patchogue Advance*, July 10, 1931; Mowry, "Listening to the Rumrunners," 13.
32. NicKenzie Lawson, *Smugglers, Bootleggers, and Scofflaws*, 19–20.
33. Willoughby, *Rum War at Sea*, 12.
34. Ibid., 105.

1921

35. "East Ender to Be Quizzed," *Port Jefferson Echo*, October 15, 1921.

1922

36. "Swears Officer Was Rum Runner," *Suffolk County News*, December 1, 1922.
37. "Troopers Get Good Whiskey," *County Review*, November 17, 1922.
38 "Fines Imposed in 'Hootch' Cases," *County Review*, November 17, 1922.
39. Ibid.
40. Ibid.

1923

41. "Amza W. Biggs Dies, Was Former Sheriff, Local Police Chief," *Long Islander*, August 8, 1957.
42. Ibid.
43. "Bootleggers Won 'Battle' Monday," *County Review*, June 22, 1923.
44. "Attempted Hold-up at Springs, Sunday," *County Review*, December 28, 1923.
45. "Girl Fought Rum Runners," *Suffolk County News*, July 27, 1923.
46. Ibid.
47. "Bootleg Gossip," *Long Islander*, September 7, 1923.

48. "Held as Rum Runners," *Long Islander*, December 14, 1923.
49. "Town Talk," *Suffolk County News*, December 14, 1923.
50. Rafferty, *Scotch on the Rocks*.
51. Ibid.
52. Ibid.

1924

53. "Held for Fourth Time as Rum-Runner," *New York Times*, December 9, 1924.
54. "To Get After the Christmas Rum-Runners," *County Review*, December 5, 1924.
55. "Much Liquor Seized in Suffolk in March," *County Review*, April 11, 1924.
56. "Bootleggers of L.I. Scored by Rev. Brown," *County Review*, February 1, 1924.
57. "Nine Drowned on Fire Island Bar," *Suffolk County News*, January 4, 1924; "Nine Men Drowned at Fire Island Inlet," *Southampton Press*, January 10, 1924; "Five Bodies Recovered," *Suffolk County News*, January 11, 1924.
58. "Seize 119 Cases of Liquor at Eastport," *County Review*, March 7, 1924.
59. "Bootleggers Lose 70 Cases of Scotch," *County Review*, January 18, 1924.
60. "$250 a Day Reasonable Rental for Motorboat," *County Review*, May 16, 1924.
61. "Oil Tank Car Full of Liquor," *East Hampton Star*, April 4, 1924.
62. "Rum Boat Sunk Off Montauk Point," *East Hampton Star*, August 8, 1924.
63. Ibid. Eccleston, who owned a string of movie theaters across Long Island, was in the newspapers twice before, once for a lawsuit trying to recover the rental fees on his very fast speedboat. He was a survivor of a boating accident in which nine men lost their lives during a terrible storm in Fire Island Inlet; gossip whispered but did not prove that perhaps rumrunning was perhaps involved.
64. "Agents Seized Wilson's Truck," *East Hampton Star*, May 9, 1924.
65. "$40,000 For Rum Runner," *East Hampton Star*, April 11, 1924.
66. "Seize Rum Craft," *East Hampton Star*, April 11, 1924.
67. "Rothstein Held after Auto Crash," *East Hampton Star*, December 12, 1924.
68. "Village and Town News," *East Hampton Star*, April 25, 1924.
69. "Alleged Rum Runners Near Smithtown," *Long Islander*, July 18, 1924.

70. "Complaint That Traffic Cop Downs Is Too Severe," *Southampton Press*, May 15, 1924.
71. "Special Constable Killed at Eastport," *County Review*, May 23, 1924; "Officer Downs Shot, Killed By Rum Runner," *Suffolk County News*, May 23, 1924; "5,000 Attend Downs' Funeral," *East Hampton Star*, May 23, 1924.
72. "Enforcement Agents Made Many Seizures on Montauk Road Last Week-End," *East Hampton Star*, November 28, 1924.
73. "Firemen Do Good Work in Downs Murder Case," *Long Islander*, May 23, 1924.
74. "Enforcement Agents Made Many Seizures on Montauk Road."
75. "Get 500 Cases Liquor at Montauk," *East Hampton Star*, May 23, 1924.
76. Ibid.
77. Ibid.
78. "First Successful Raid Made on Bootleggers at Montauk," *East Hampton Star*, February 29, 1924; "Raid Rum Runners at Fort Pond Bay," *Southampton Express*, March 6, 1924; "First Successful Raid Made on Bootleggers," *Southampton Press*, March 6, 1924.
79. "Prohibition Men Now Hunt by Scent," *Suffolk County News*, March 14, 1924.
80. Ibid. The newspaper article noted that two trucks captured between Eastport and Patchogue were owned by Mercier & Liebel Sunrise Train Transportation of Patchogue. Two more belonged to W.K. Homes's Inter-City Transportation Company also of Patchogue. The last large truck was a private vehicle that belonged to a Greenport resident. The author does not say whether the trucks were rented, stolen or if the owners knew what they were being used for.
81. "Rum Running Not As Profitable As Before," *Southampton Press*, April 10, 1924.
82. Ibid.
83. Ibid.
84. "Most Profitable Industry Is Booze," *Suffolk County News*, November 14, 1924.
85. Ibid.
86. Ibid.
87. Ibid.
88. Ibid.
89. "Hazards of Rum Running," *Suffolk County News*, November 28, 1924. After word of this story was seen by federal officials, this station underwent an investigation and the crew was split up and sent to other postings. A new, more "dry" crew was moved to the station.

90. "Hazards of Rum Running."

91. "Traps Rum Craft on His First Night," *New York Times*, August 7, 1924; "Greenport Woman Exposed Rum Ring," *Suffolk County News*, October 2, 1925.

1925

92. "Patrol Boat Fires Upon Five Persons at Mattituck," *County Review*, April 30, 1925.

93. "Riverhead Man Held Up at Point of Revolver," *County Review*, April 9, 1925.

94. Rafferty, *Scotch on the Rocks.*

95. "To Move Coast Guard Base," *New York Times*, August 30, 1925

96. "Seize Italian Ship as Liquor Suspect," *New York Times*, January 2, 1925; "Rum Running Still in Progress," *Long Islander*, January 9, 1925; "More Side Lights on Rum Running," *Long Islander*, April 17, 1925; "Schooner Is Held by Customs Men," *New York Times*, January 3, 1925; "Rum Schooner's Crew Found Guilty," *New York Times*, April 2, 1925.

97. "More Side Lights of Rum Running"; "Rum Runners Car Wrecked on Turnpike," *Long Islander*, January 16, 1925.

98. "Is Rum Running on the Wane?" *Long Islander*, April 17, 1925.

99. "Thieves Visit Westhampton In Epidemic of Island Robberies," *Suffolk County News*, November 20, 1925; *Port Jefferson Echo*, November 26, 1925; *East Hampton Star*, October 16, 1925; "Rum Running Is Not Yet Dead," *Southampton Press*, April 30, 1925.

100. "Revive Montauk Hijacking Case," *Patchogue Advance*, December 3, 1926.

101. "Jury Disagrees in Hijacking Case," *County Review*, June 18, 1925.

102. Ibid.

103. "Four Indicted by Federal Grand Jury," *Southampton Press*, May 14, 1925; "Jury Disagrees in Hijacking Case"; "Re-open Montauk Highjack Case," *East Hampton Star*, May 21, 1926.

104. "Spotlight at Last on L.I. Rum Scandal," *Suffolk County News*, April 17, 1925.

105. "Jury Disagrees in Hijacking Case."

106. "Spotlight at Last on L.I. Rum Scandal."

107. "Jury Disagrees in Hijacking Case."

108. "Spotlight at Last on L.I. Rum Scandal."

109. "Grand Jury Indicts Hijackers on Charge of Burglary," *County Review*, May 7, 1925.

110. Ibid.; "Revive Montauk Hijacking Case"'; "Revive Montauk Hijacking Case," *East Hampton Star*, December 10, 1926; "Drop Montauk Rum Charges," *County Review*, March 10, 1927.

111. "Patchogue," *Suffolk County News*, April 24, 1925; "Jury in Hijacking Case Disagrees After Deliberating for Three Hours," *County Review*, June 18, 1925; "Rum Probe Witnesses Disclaim All Knowledge of Bootlegging," *East Hampton Star*, April 24, 1925.

112. "Seize Schooner Find Rum Aboard," *East Hampton Star*, August 7, 1925.

113. "Load of Rye Is Seized in Suffolk," *East Hampton Star*, January 9, 1925.

114. "Stops Speeder-Finds Rum," *East Hampton Star*, January 9, 1925.

115. "Movie Players Mistaken for Rum Running Crew," *Southampton Press*, January 8, 1925.

1926

116. "Greenport Woman Exposed Rum Ring," *Suffolk County News*, October 2, 1925.

117. Ibid.

118. "Rum-Runner's Wife Gave Clue for Raid on Broadway Ring," *New York Times*, September 27, 1925; "Hans Furhmann Dies Mysteriously after Bootleg Ring Trial," *County Review*, February 11, 1926.

119. "Boat Seized as Rum Suspect," *East Hampton Star*, March 12, 1926.

120. "Message Washed Ashore," *Suffolk County News*, July 16, 1926.

1927

121. "Troopers Make Rum Seizure," *East Hampton Star*, April 1, 1927; "Claim Hijackers Gave Raid Tip," *Patchogue Advance*, April 1, 1927.

122. "Sub Chaser Now Rum Runner," *East Hampton Star*, April 1, 1927.

123. "Haley and Pitts Held in Rum Case," *East Hampton Star*, January 21, 1927.

124. "Wholesale Outbreak of Automobile Stealing," *Patchogue Advance*, November 1, 1927.

125. "Wild Waves Saying, 'Yo Ho and a Bottle of Rum,'" *Suffolk County News*, April 20, 1927.

1928

126. "Coast Guard Wounded," *Suffolk County News*, November 30, 1928.
127. "Five Days in Jail for Selling Liquor," *Suffolk County News*, April 20, 1928.
128. "Guy Fawks [*sic*] Hanged at Round Pond," *Sag Harbor Express*, December 21, 1928.

1929

129. "'Marjorie' and Crew Caught in Running Battle," *East Hampton Star*, December 6, 1929; "Nab Rum Runner Near Montauk," *Suffolk County News*, December 6, *1929*.
130. "Two Rum Runners Captured Sunday," *Patchogue Advance*, December 31, 1929; "Coast Guard Boats Active," *Suffolk County News*, January 3, 1930.
131. "Two Rum Runners Captured Sunday."
132. "Police Frustrate Rum Landing Here," *Patchogue Advance*, December 10, 1929.
133. Ibid.
134. "Seize $10,000 Load of Liquor," *Suffolk County News*, December 13, 1929.
135. "35 Simultaneous Raids," *Suffolk County News*, October 18, 1929.

1930

136. "9 Rum Runner Get Stiff Terms," *East Hampton Star*, April 10, 1931; "2 Big Liquor Ships Taken off Montauk," *County Review*, January 1, 1931.
137. "3 Slain in Dry Raid on Rum Runners Sunday A.M.," *East Hampton Star*, January 3, 1930; "Why Not Play the Game Fairly?" *Suffolk County News*, January 3, 1930; "Jury on Rum Killing Absolves Coast Guard," *New York Times*, January 15, 1930; "Dry Men Get *Black Duck*," *New York Times*, March 7, 1930; "Upholds Coast Guard in *Black Duck* Killing," *New York Times*, January 17, 1930. While the vessel was docked in Providence, a guard, Edward Foley from the Internal Revenue Service, was assigned to keep the curious crowd back from the boat. Foley, who had been selected because of his spotless record, had gone to a nearby boat and claimed he needed a small bottle of liquor because of a bad cold. Misjudging the effect of booze after abstinence, Foley quickly became very drunk and

menaced the crowd with a pair of pistols, weaving on his feet. When he fell, the small bottle of liquor in his pocket shattered. When he regained his feet, he shoved his pistol into the stomach of Gilbert Taylor. Taylor managed to gain control of the weapon and, along with Richard Rathbun, convinced Foley to go to a nearby shed. There Foley called his office and claimed that a gang of hijackers were about to attack the ship and that it was the second time the ship was attacked. After Foley made his claims, Taylor borrowed the phone and put in a call to authorities, explaining the situation at the *Black Duck*. Foley was suspended and told to go sleep it off. "More Liquor Found on Patrol Boats," *New York Times*, January 6, 1930.

138. "Insufficient Evidence Frees Coast Guard from Assault Charge," *East Hampton Star*, February 21, 1930. The other members of the group that were stopped were Mr. and Mrs. Benjamin H. Barnes, Mr. and Mrs. William Young, Mr. and Mrs. Fred H. Scribner and Mr. and Mrs. Leonard Edwards. Born in Patterson, New Jersey, Alexander Blue moved to Suffolk County in 1904. He was elected to the chief prosecutor's job in 1930, when Hildreth stepped down. He served until 1932 and led a vigorous fight against bootleggers—so vigorous that the Republicans refused to renominate him for the job. After that, Blue retired from active politics.

139. "Insufficient Evidence Frees Coast Guard from Assault Charge."

140. "Trawler *Notus* Taken in Custody by C.G," *East Hampton Star*, February 14, 1930; "Insufficient Evidence Frees Coast Guard from Assault Charge." The later article states that Commander Sullivan, in charge of the area, identified the wrong Coast Guard ship. Sullivan identified the ship as the Coast Guard ship *Downes*, when it actually was the Coast Guard ship *Nimaha*.

141. "Harry Bowen, 300 Foot Collier Piled on Rocks off Montauk Beach," *East Hampton Star*, November 21, 1930.

142. "Tractor and Trailer Liquor Outfit Seized on Beach," *Patchogue Advance*, June 3, 1930; "West Sayville Boat Is Seized," *Suffolk County News*, June 6 1930.

143. "West Sayville Boat Is Seized"; "Rum Running Outfit Is Seized at Beach," *Patchogue Advance*, June 3, 1930.

144. "Rum Schooner Captured," *East Hampton Star*, October 24, 1930.

145. Ibid.

146. Ibid.

147. "Rum Boats Seized by the Coast Guard Lately," *East Hampton Star*, September 26, 1930; "Rum Boats Seized by the Coast Guard," *Patchogue Advance*, September 23, 1930.

148. "Rum Boats Seized by the Coast Guard Lately"; "Rum Boats Seized by the Coast Guard."

149. "Potatoes Used as Blind for Cargo of Contraband Wet Goods Taken in Daylight," *Patchogue Advance*, April 1, 1930.

150. "Big Rum Seizure Is Made in Islip Creek," *Patchogue Advance*, October 21, 1930. The men arrested were Morris Lovinson-Levine of Freeport, Sam Bender of Manhattan, John Anderson of Merrick, Herman Alter of Hempstead, Elmer Jones and Archie Scarborough of Brightwaters, Allen Austin of Brooklyn, George Dunn of Bay Shore, Jack Miller of Manhattan and Alexander Bawers of Lake Ronkonkoma.

151. "Wilson's Home Linked to Diamond's Case," *Patchogue Advance*, October 21, 1930.

152. "Rum Flows to City in Motor Caravan," *Patchogue Advance*, March 4, 1930.

153. "Says Rum Runners Set Up Reign of Terror on River," *Patchogue Advance*, January 10, 1930.

154. "Two Rum Boats Are Caught Off Montauk Point," *Patchogue Advance*, February 25, 1930.

155. Ibid.; "Catch Two Rum Boats," *Suffolk County News*, February 28, 1930.

156. "Sharp Onslaught Has Given Liquor Runners a Pause," *Patchogue Advance*, April 15, 1930.

157. Ibid.

158. "Seize 2 Truck Loads of Liquor," *Suffolk County News*, April 4, 1930.

159. Ibid.

160. "Brewery in Operation Here Is Raided and Stuff Dumped," *Patchogue Advance*, June 10, 1930.

161. "Broere's Bail Fixed at $3,000," *Suffolk County News*, April 18, 1930.

162. "West Sayville Man Sent to Jail for Rum Running with Gang," *Patchogue Advance*, September 16, 1930.

163. "Bootleg Radios Are Raided by U.S. Men," *Patchogue Advance*, July 22, 1930; "Seize 'Bootleg' Sets," *Suffolk County News*, July 25, 1930.

164. "Seize Large Load of Liquor," *Suffolk County News*, March 14, 1930.

165. Ibid.

166. "Transfer Load of Rum Right on Main Road?" *Patchogue Advance*, August 26, 1930.

167. "Two Breweries Are Raided Over Week-end," *Patchogue Advance*, September 9, 1930.

168. Ibid.

169. "Four Patchoguers Are Caught in U.S. Roundup of Island Branch of Big Rum Syndicate," *Patchogue Advance*, September 9, 1930.

170. "Lack of Tail Light Undoing of Potato-Rum Enterprise," *Patchogue Advance*, September 30, 1930.

171. "Blue and Two Officers Fight Pistol Battle in Speeding Cars with Desperate Rum Runners," *Patchogue Advance*, November 25, 1930.

172. Ibid.; "Dist. Atty. and His Men in Gun Fight with Rum Runners," *Suffolk County News*, November 28, 1930.

173. "To Investigate Liquor Seizure," *Suffolk County News*, December 5, 1930.

174. "Catch Two Liquor Loads Same Place within 12 Hours," *Patchogue Advance*, December 12, 1930.

175. "Rum Boat Rammed Off Fire Island," *Suffolk County News*, December 19, 1930.

176. Ibid.

177. "Honest Load of Spuds Makes Heavy Job for Doubting Troopers," *Patchogue Advance*, December 26, 1930.

178. "Suffolk Votes for Change in Dry Law," *Patchogue Advance*, September 30, 1930.

1931

179. Conversation with Carl D. Reiter Jr., Mattituck Library, 2018.

180. "'Artemis' Rum Boat Is Found," *County Review*, August 27, 1931; "District Attorney's Weekly Bulletin," *East Hampton Star*, August 28, 1931; "Coast Guard Shot Up Boat," *Watchman of the Sunrise Trail*, August 27, 1931; "Activities of District Attorney A.G. Blue," *Long Islander*, August 28, 1931; "Crippled Rum Boat Turns Up at Local Yard for Repairs," *Port Jefferson Times-Echo*, August 28, 1931.

181. "Crippled Rum Boat Turns Up at Local Yard for Repairs."

182. Ibid.

183. "Contracts Let for Erection of Two New School Buildings in Suffolk," *Suffolk County News*, September 18, 1931.

184. "Find Rum Hoard and Wireless," *Suffolk County News*, December 18, 1931.

185. "Crew of Rum Yacht Gets Light Penalty," *New York Times*, December 17, 1931; "A Magnificent Yacht Caught as a Smuggler," *Patchogue Advance*, July 3, 1931.

186. "$8000 More Bail on Branding Witnesses," *Patchogue Advance*, July 17, 1931; "Man and Woman Are Arrested in Bootleg Torture Case"; "Many Brief Island Notes," *Patchogue Advance*, September 4, 1931; "The First

of Alleged Torturers Acquitted," *Patchogue Advance*, November 27, 1931; "Men Were Branded with Hot Irons in Hijacking Feud."

187. "Find Rum Hoard and Wireless."

188. "Rum Ship Seized in Fort Pond Bay," *Suffolk County News*, January 30, 1931.

189. "Funeral Brought About Capture of Rum Running Boat," *Patchogue Advance*, August 4, 1931; "Coast Guards on Way to Funeral Nab Rum Runners," *Long Islander*, August 7, 1931.

190. "Diamond Hookup in This County?" *Patchogue Advance*, May 5, 1931.

191. "Halls at Yaphank and Medford Are Raided by U.S. Dry Officers," *Patchogue Advance*, May 5, 1931.

192. Ibid.

193. "Drastic Shakeup in Coast Guard," *Suffolk County News*, January 15, 1932.

1932

194. "$1,000 Bribery Trap Sprung in Suffolk," *New York Times*, May 1, 1932; "3 Nabbed in Cutchogue Booze Raid," *County Review*, May 5, 1932.

195. Pilar, "Rum Smugglers Use Decoy to Fool Guard."

196. Rafferty, *Scotch on the Rocks*.

197. "Drastic Shakeup in Coast Guard," *Suffolk County News*, January 15, 1932.

198. "'Big Shots' of Bootlegging Are Booked for Trial," *Patchogue Advance*, April 8, 1932; "Koman Indicted as Rum Briber," *Suffolk County News*, April 8, 1932.

199. "Coast Guardsman Is Shot as Rum Shipment Is Seized," *Suffolk County News*, May 13, 1932.

200. "Seize Illegal Radio," *Patchogue Advance*, May 13, 1932.

201. "Gustave Fischel Made Mayor of Babylon, Filling Vacancy," *Patchogue Advance*, June 3, 1932; "Policemen Held in Raid," *New York Times*, May 13, 1932.

202. "Rum Boats Caught," *Patchogue Advance*, December 30, 1932.

203. Hausrath, "Bayman's Random Harvest."

Other Remembrances

204. Rich, *Memoir*, 23.
205. Dickinson, interview, August 22, 2002, copy held at the Southold Historical Society, Southold, Suffolk County, New York, 25.
206. Gilbert and Askcin, interview, August 27, 2002, copy held at the Southold Historical Museum, Southold, Suffolk County, New York, 21–22.
207. Conversation with anonymous member of the Southold DAR.
208. "Johnnie Piccozzi and Rum running," unpublished files of the Southold Historical Museum, n.d.
209. Ibid.
210. Conversation with Herb Strobel and Richard Wines of Hallockville Museum Farm, 2018.

Code Book

211. Ambrose—this entry probably refers to the Ambrose Lightship.
212. Atlantic Highland Mandaley Pier—Atlantic Highlands is north and west of Sandy Hook along the same bay. In 1905, a ferry service using the SS *Mandalay* was started from Atlantic Highlands to New York City. The ferry ran three times a day and lasted until the 1940s. The pier was replaced in the twentieth century with the municipal harbor.
213. Ambrose Channel is off Sandy Hook, New Jersey.
214. Approximately twenty-three miles long, the creek is a tributary of the Delaware River in New Jersey. Named after an Indian chief, Alloway Creek is located in southern New Jersey, next to the Delaware border.
215. Arsonel warf at Pensgrove [*sic*] (Arsenal wharf at Penn's Grove). Penn's Grove is a small village in New Jersey on the Delaware border that was founded in the early 1800s, active in shipping farm freight to Wilmington and Philadelphia.
216. Absecon or Atlantic City. Absecon, New Jersey, was created in 1872 from Egg Harbor township and Galloway township. Named "Little Stream' in the Absegami language, the city is located along the Absecon Bay west of Atlantic City, which located at the mouth of the bay.
217. Barnagat. Located in New Jersey, Barnegat Light, formerly known as Barnegat City, is a borough on the barrier beach that protects Barnegat Bay in eastern New Jersey. The code book may be referring to Barnegat Lighthouse, which is located on the barrier beach.

218. Belford. In New Jersey, Belford is located along Sandy Hook Bay and sits almost directly opposite Staten Island and the entrance to New York Harbor.

219. Bergen Point is in Bayonne, New Jersey, and comprises the southern tip of Constable Hook.

220. Block Island is a small island off Long Island and Rhode Island.

221. U.S. Lightship *Barnegat* was built in 1904 in Camden, New Jersey. It worked as a lightship from 1904 to 1924 in the Five Fathom Bank area. In 1927, it was moved to the Barnegat Lighthouse station, where it remained until 1942.

222. Bodie Island. Nags Head, North Carolina, part of the Outer Banks barrier beaches just to the east of Roanoke Island.

223. Cliffwood, New Jersey. Tucked along the coast line of Raritan Bay, Cliffwood is opposite State Island.

224. Chalk Works. Possibly Edinburgh, United Kingdom.

225. Cataret ferry [*sic*]. Carteret, New Jersey, is located on the shores of Arthur Kill across from State Island.

226. Cohansey River. In southern New Jersey, the river, which starts in Bridgeton, winds its way to the Delaware River.

227. Cape Henlopen Point. A small out cropping of land in Delaware at the mouth of the Delaware River across from Cape May, New Jersey.

228. Cape May Point. A small peninsula at the southernmost tip of New Jersey.

229. Cape Cod. The large peninsula in southern Massachusetts that juts out in an L shape into the Atlantic Ocean.

230. Coney Island Creek. A creek that partially divides Seagate and Brighton Beach from the rest of Brooklyn.

231. Chesapeake Light Ship. One of several lightships named the *Chesapeake* that has existed since 1820. The current ship was launched in 1930 and worked until the 1960s. The ship was stationed in the Chesapeake Bay area.

232. Cape Charles is toward the end of a peninsula that starts in Delaware but is part of Virginia. The town is along the inner section of the peninsula that faces Chesapeake Bay and is across from Newport News and Norfolk.

233. Cape Henry. At the mouth of the Chesapeake Bay area is Cape Henry on the shore of Virginia Beach, Virginia. The Cape Henry Lighthouse in nearby Fort Story was built in 1881 and has a distinctive black-and-white-striped body.

234. Currituck Beach Light. Standing on the outer Banks of North Carolina, the Currituck Beach light stands in Corolla, North Carolina, on what was

once a separate island from Bodie Island. The light, which is distinctive because it was never painted, has an even brown body.

235. Cape Hatteras is near the tip of one of the barrier beaches protecting Pamlico Sound from the ocean in North Carolina. The area is marked with a black-and-white-striped lighthouse.

236. Deadman Shoal Light. Marking a deadly shoal near the mouth of the Delaware River, Deadman Shoal was marked on the northeast side by a lighthouse.

237. Delaware River. Starting in the Catskill Mountains of New York, most of the river course marks the border between New Jersey, Pennsylvania and Delaware.

238. Dennis Creek. A small waterway that flows into the Delaware River close to its junction with the Atlantic Ocean.

239. Diamond Shoals Light Ship. Located off Cape Hatteras, the Diamond Shoals light ship (LV71) has the distinction of being the only lightship to be sunk by enemy fire in U.S. waters during World War I. Six lightships marked the shoals until 1966, when a "Texas Tower"–style lighthouse was erected on the shoals.

240. Egg Island Point. Just inside the mouth of the Delaware River, Egg Island Point is a small peninsula in New Jersey and sits to the north and west of Cape May.

241. Fort Hamilton. Named after a military fort established in the early 1800s. Fort Hamilton marks the mouth of New York Harbor and is also the site of the eastern side of the Verrazano Narrows Bridge.

242. Fort Wadsworth. Opposite Fort Hamilton, the site was first used by the Dutch in 1636 for a blockhouse to guard the narrow entrance to New York Harbor. The site is also the western side of the Verrazano Narrows Bridge.

243. Fryes Dock. Location unknown.

244. Five Fathom lightship. Close to fifteen miles off of Cape May, the lightship marked Five Fathom Bank. The ship was eventually replaced in 1972 with a horn buoy.

245. Ferry wharf at Pensgrove [sic]. Penns Grove is located on the eastern bank of the Delaware River in southwestern New Jersey. The community sits opposite Wilmington, Delaware.

246. Fire Island Light Ship. Lightship number 114 was built in Portland, Oregon, and has the distinction of being the first lightship to travel from the West Coast to the East, when it was assigned to a site off the south shore of Long Island, New York. The lightship was stationed at Fire Island from 1930 to 1942.

247. Fenwick Shoal Light Ship. Lightship number 116 was stationed for three years, 1930–33, at Fenwick Shoals off the Fenwick Island, Delaware. Fenwick Island is part of the barrier beaches on the border between Delaware and Maryland.

248. Fire Island Inlet. Located on Long Island, New York's south shore, Fire Island Inlet is part of the overlapping barrier beaches that lead to the Great South Bay.

249. Great Beds Red. Great Beds lies off between the southern edge of Staten Island and New Jersey at the edge of Raritan Bay.

250. Saint Pierre and Miquelon. A small group of islands off the southern coast of Newfoundland.

251. Liverpool N.S. Liverpool, Nova Scotia, is located along the Atlantic coastline, a center for rumrunning shippers during the 1920s. The business bolstered the small community's economy until a paper mill was built.

252. Halifax N.S. On the eastern side of a protected peninsula in Nova Scotia, Halifax is a major business center in the area.

253. Lunenburg. Located on the southern coast of Nova Scotia, Lunenburg was a farm and fishing community that specialized in boatbuilding and repair especially during World War I.

254. Highlands. Along the innermost edge of Sandy Hook Bay in New Jersey, Highlands is nestled behind a narrow barrier beach that leads to Gateway National Recreation Area.

255. Harrison. Just east of Newark, Harrison sits along the Passaic River in New Jersey.

256. Halifax N.S. On the eastern side of a protected peninsula in Nova Scotia, Halifax is a major business center in the area.

257. Hog Island Light. Built in 1896, the Hog Island Light on the Virginia Barrier Islands was an octagonal iron skeleton tower, which replaced an 1853 structure. Abandoned in 1948, the structure was demolished.

258. Jack Knife Bridge. Possibly Jack Knife Bascule Bridge in Thunder Bay, Ontario. The bridge spans the Kaministiquia River just before it empties into Lake Superior.

259. Jake's dock. Location unknown.

260. Jones Inlet. Located at the west end of Jones Beach, a barrier beach protecting the south shore of Long Island, New York. The inlet is bracketed by the community of Port Lookout to the west and Jones Beach State Park to the east.

261. Kasbay Brick Yard. Location unknown.

262. Keansburg. Between Raritan Bay and Sandy Hook Bay, Keansburg, New Jersey, is opposite Staten Island, New York.

263. Keyport. On the south side of Raritan Bay, Keyport is tucked behind the peninsula of Union Beach, New Jersey

264. Liverpool, N.S. On the ocean side of the Nova Scotia peninsula and roughly level with Maine.

265. Monument #1 Flashing White. Location unknown

266. Monument #2 Flashing Green. Location unknown.

267. Monument #3 Flashing White. Location unknown.

268. Monument #4 Flashing Red. Location unknown.

269. Monument #5 Flashing White. Location unknown.

270. Morgan. Possibly Morgan Bay along the Maine Coast, close to Blue Hill and Mount Desert Island.

271. Mill Creek. Empties into Lewis Bay on Cape Cod, Massachusetts.

272. Mad Horse. Mad Horse Creek opens on to the Delaware River in southwestern New Jersey.

273. Montauk Point. The eastern tip of the south fork of Long Island, New York

274. Nantucket Shoal Light Ship. Forty miles southeast of the island of Nantucket, the Nantucket shoals has had a lightship stationed at its southern edge since 1854.

275. Northeast End Light Ship. Stationed in Delaware Bay, New Jersey, at Five Fathom Bank, a lightship has been stationed in the northeast end area of the navigational hazard since 1882.

276. Occ. An abbreviation that stands for occulting light, which is a light that flashes in a pattern where the time when it flashes on is longer than when it is dark. This type of light pattern is typically used in lighthouses and on navigational buoys. Occ. No 6 Red Gong—possibly Musselbed shoals in Narraganset Bay, Portsmouth, Rhode Island.

277. Occ. No. 12 Red. Ambrose Channel Rear Range Light area, Staten Island.

278. Occ. No. 15 Green. Location unknown.

279. Occ. No. 18 Red Gong. Location unknown.

280. Occ. No. 26 Red Bell. Gowanus Flats, in the upper bay of New York Harbor, just west of Brooklyn.

281. Old Orchard. Probably Old Orchard Beach, Maine, located on Saco Bay in southern Maine. The area took its name from an abandoned apple orchard left behind by the Rogers family in the 1630s. It is said that the orchard survived on its own for 150 years.

282. Overfalls Light Ship. The Overfall shoal is located midpoint between Cape May, New Jersey, and Cape Henlopen, Delaware. A lightship was first assigned to the area in 1898. Four ships were anchored there until 1960, when a channel marker buoy took over the job.
283. Penn R.R. Bridge. There are nine bridges that are referred to as the Pennsylvania Railroad Bridge. In this case, the bridge is probably referring to the Pennsylvania Railroad Bridge at Columbia, Pennsylvania, over the Susquehanna River.
284. Port Newark. Directly west of Staten Island, the waters of Newark Bay connect with the Hackensack River and the upper bay of New York Harbor as well as Arthur Kill, Kill van Kull and Raritan Bay.
285. Shrewsbury Rock light. A lighted buoy, Shrewsbury Rock light marks the eastern end of a rocky shoal off the coast of New Jersey just south of Sandy Hook.
286. Asbury Park. On the New Jersey shoreline, Asbury Park is south of Sandy Hook and Long Island, along the New York/New Jersey Bight (the Atlantic Ocean).
287. Sea Breeze dock. Location unknown.
288. Sea Girt light. Along the New Jersey sea coast, Sea Girt is south of Asbury Park and north of Barnegat Bay. The light marks the entrance to a body of water named Wrecking Pond. The light was not established until 1896. The light was automated in 1945 and deactivated in 1977.
289. Cape Cod Highland Light. Located on the Cape Cod National Seashore, the lighthouse is now known as the Highland Light. Built in 1857, the light is the oldest and tallest lighthouse in the area. It replaced two other earlier towers. The light sits close to the northern tip of Cape Cod.
290. Sankaty Head Light. Located on Nantucket Island in the village of Siasconset, the light was built in 1850 and automated in 1965.
291. Gay Head Light. Located in Martha's Vineyard in Aquinnah, Massachusetts, the current light was built in 1856. The light was automated in the mid-1950s. Due to erosion, the lighthouse was relocated 129 feet away from its original location in 2015.
292. Montauk Point Light. Built in 1796, the light marks the southern tip of Long Island. The light was extended in height from 80 feet to just over 110 feet in 1860. The light was electrified in 1940 and automated in 1987.
293. Ambrose Light Ship. Anchored in the Ambrose channel off Sandy Hook, New Jersey. The first lightship was anchored in the channel in 1823 as a navigation aid to shipping entering New York Harbor. Over the years,

several lightships all called the *Ambrose* were stationed in the channel and remained until 1967.

294. Scotland Light Ship. Also known as the Ambrose Lightship (see Ambrose Lightship)

295. Romer Shoals. Named after a pilot boat, the *William J. Romer*, which sank in 1863, the shoal in New Jersey's waters is located in Lower New York Bay and marked with a small lighthouse. It is on the northern edge of the Swash channel and close by to Ambrose Channel and Sandy Hook, New Jersey.

296. Robbins Reef. Just off Constable Hook in Bayonne, New Jersey, Robbins Reef is a small ridge of sand that is marked with a small lighthouse that was built in 1883 to replace an earlier 1839 tower.

297. Raritan Bay. The southwestern section of lower New York Bay, the bay is surrounded by New Jersey, Staten Island and the Atlantic Ocean. The bay is named for local Native Americans who lived in the area.

298. Rockaway Inlet. The body of water that connects Jamaica Bay with the Atlantic Ocean. The inlet has Brooklyn to the north and Rockaway Peninsula to the south.

299. Sea Girt. Along the New Jersey sea coast, Sea Girt is south of Asbury Park and north of Barnegat Bay.

300. Scotland. Located on the southern end of Maryland. Scotland is located on the western shore of Chesapeake Bay.

301. Shrewsbury Rock. A rocky shoal off the coast of New Jersey just south of Sandy Hook.

302. Sandy Hook. A narrow peninsula that juts out into lower New York Harbor. The land is the northernmost end of the New Jersey shore barrier beaches.

303. Sandy Hook Point. The northernmost end of Sandy Hook. Most of the north end of the peninsula is occupied by Fort Hancock, a sprawling fort that was established in 1896. Part of the fort was transformed into the Sand Hook Proving Grounds and was used until 1919, when the U.S. Army decided to relocate.

304. South River. South River in New Jersey connects to the Raritan River close to Raritan Bay

305. South Channel. Located in Sayreville, New Jersey, in the Raritan River.

306. South Amboy. Along the south shore of the Raritan River just as it widens into Raritan Bay.

307. Seawaren Dock. Located in Sewaren, New Jersey, between Perth Amboy and Carteret, the community is across from Staten Island. The area had and currently has a number of docks.

308. Sea Breeze Point. A short peninsula along the Delaware River across from Bombay Hook National Wildlife Refuge.

309. Stow Creek. An area along the Delaware River on the New Jersey side midway between Wilmington and Dover, Delaware.

310. Ship John light. This small lighthouse is situated on the north side of Delaware Bay near Bombay Hook National Wildlife Refuge. Built in 1877, the light was automated in 1973. The light was named after the ship *John*, which sunk on the site while on a voyage from Hamburg, Germany, to Philadelphia in 1797.

311. Salem Creek. Location unknown.

312. Shinnecock Light. Located on the south fork of Long Island, New York. The Shinnecock light was built in 1858 and was deactivated in 1931, when a skeleton tower was installed. The original brick tower was demolished in 1948.

313. Saint Pierre and Miquelon. A small group of islands off the southern coast of Newfoundland.

314. Shark River. Between Avon by the Sea and Belmar, New Jersey, Shark River flows into an estuary that empties into the ocean. Originally called the Nolletquesset, the river has also been called the Shirk and Shack River.

315. Woodbridge Creek. Empties into Arthur Kill, from the New Jersey side, close to the Outerbridge Crossing bridge between New Jersey and New York.

316. Whistle Buoy No. 2. Location unknown

317. Whistle Buoy No. 4. Either a buoy in Portland Harbor, Maine, or a buoy off Southwest Point, Block Island, Rhode Island.

318. Whistle Buoy No. 6. Marks a rock southeast of the Petit Manan Island in Maine.

319. Winter Quarter Shoal Light Ship. Anchored approximately eight and a half miles off of Assateague Island, Virginia, the lightship was first assigned to the area in 1874. A lightship served the area until 1960. The lightship was then replaced by a lighted buoy.

320. Zachs Inlet. A small bay nestled along the north side of Jones Beach State Park, just off South Oyster Bay, and south of Wantagh, New York.

BIBLIOGRAPHY

Bramson, Ruthann, Geoffrey K. Fleming and Amy Kasuga Folk. *A World Unto Itself: The Remarkable History of Plum Island, New York.* Southold, NY: Southold Historical Society, 2014.

Carson, Gerald. *Old Country Store.* New York: Oxford University Press, 1954.

Clark, Norman. *Deliver Us from Evil, An Interpretation of American Prohibition.* New York: W.W. Norton and Co., 1976.

County Review. "'Artemis' Rum Boat Is Found." August 27, 1931, 1.

———. "Attempted Hold-Up at Springs, Sunday." December 28, 1923.

———. "Bootleggers Lose 70 Cases of Scotch." January 18, 1924.

———. "Bootleggers of L.I. Scored by Rev. Brown." February 1, 1924.

———. "Bootleggers Won 'Battle' Monday." June 22, 1923, 1.

———. "Drop Montauk Rum Charges; Court Frees Defendants." March 10, 1927, 1.

———. "Fines Imposed in 'Hootch' Cases." November 17, 1922.

———. "Grand Jury Indicts Hijackers on Charge of Burglary, First Degree." May 7, 1925, 1, 2.

———. "Hans Furhmann Dies Mysteriously after Bootleg Ring Trial." February 11, 1926, 1.

———. "Jury Disagrees in Hijacking Case." June 18, 1925, 1, 3.

———. "Jury Indicts Hijackers On Charge of Burglary." May 7 , 1925, 1, 2.

———. "Jury in Hijacking Case Disagrees After Deliberating for Three Hours." June 18, 1925, 1, 3.

———. "Much Liquor Seized in Suffolk in March." April 11, 1924.

———. "Patrol Boat Fires Upon Five Persons at Mattituck." April 30, 1925, 1–2.

———. "Riverhead Man Held Up at Point of Revolver." April 9, 1925, 1.

———. "Seize 119 Cases of Liquor at Eastport." March 7, 1924.

———. "Special Constable Killed at Eastport Friday Night." May 23, 1924, 1-2.

———. "3 Nabbed in Cutchogue Booze Raid." May 5, 1932, 3.

———. "To Get After the Christmas Rum-Runners." December 5, 1924, 6.

———. "Troopers Get Good Whiskey." November 17, 1922.

———. "2 Big Liquor Ships Taken off Montauk." January 1, 1931.

———. "$250 a Day Reasonable Rental for Motorboat." May 16, 1924.

Dickinson, Wes. Interview by Folklorist Steve Warick, August 22, 2002.

East Hampton Star. "Agents Seized Wilson's Truck." May 9, 1924

———. "Boat Seized as Rum Suspect." March 12, 1926, 10.

———. "District Attorney's Weekly Bulletin." August 28, 1931, 4.

———. "Enforcement Agents Made Many Seizures on Montauk Road Last Week-End; Thirteen Men and Cars." November 28, 1924, 1, 10.

———. "First Successful Raid Made on Bootleggers at Montauk." February 29, 1924, 1.

———. "5,000 Attend Downs' Funeral." May 23, 1924, 1.

———. "$40,000 For Rum Runner." April 11, 1924.

———. "Get 500 Cases Liquor at Montauk." May 23, 1924, 1.

———. "Haley and Pitts Held in Rum Case." January 21, 1927, 1.

———. "Harry Bowen, 300 Foot Collier Piled on Rocks off Montauk Beach." November 21, 1930, 1.

———. "Insufficient Evidence Frees Coast Guard from Assault Charge; Court Packed at Hearing Held Tuesday." February 21, 1930, 1, 10.

———. "Load of Rye Is Seized in Suffolk." January 9, 1925.

———. "'Marjorie' and Crew Caught in Running Battle." December 6, 1929, 1.

———. "9 Rum Runners Get Stiff Terms." April 10, 1931, 1.

———. October 16, 1925, 4.

———. "Oil Tank Car Full of Liquor." April 4, 1924

———. "Re-open Montauk Highjack Case." May 21, 1926, 1.

———. "Revive Montauk Hijacking Case." December 10, 1926, 9.

———. "Rothstein Held after Auto Crash." December 12, 1924.

———. "Rum Boats Seized by the Coast Guard Lately." September 26, 1930, 1.

———. "Rum Boat Sunk Off Montauk Point." August 8, 1924.

———. "Rum Probe Witnesses Disclaim All Knowledge of Bootlegging." April 24, 1925, 1.

———. "Rum Schooner Captured; Shots Halt Second Runner." October 24, 1930, 1.

———. "Seize Rum Craft." April 11, 1924

———. "Seize Schooner Find Rum Aboard." August 7, 1925, 1.

———. "Stops Speeder-Finds Rum." January 9, 1925, 1.

———. "Sub Chaser Now Rum Runner." April 1, 1927, 1.

———. "3 Slain in Dry Raid on Rum Runners Sunday A.M.; Lowman Defends Coast Guard, 3 Boats Caught Off Montauk." January 3, 1930, 1930.

———. "Trawler *Notus* Taken in Custody by C.G.; Find 400 Sacks of Liquor." February 14, 1930, 1.

———. "Troopers Make Rum Seizure." April 1, 1927, 1.

———. "Village and Town News." April 25, 1924

Folk, Amy Kasuga. "The General Store on Long Island, 1810–1860." Master's thesis, Long Island University, 2008.

Gilbert, Bob, and Ray Akscin. Interview by folklorist Steve Warick, August 27, 2002.

Hausrath, Ralph H. "A Bayman's Random Harvest." *Long Island Forum*, January 1975, 6–9.

"Johnnie Piccozzi." Unpublished files of the Southold Historical Museum, n.d.

Larkin, Jack. *The Reshaping of Everyday Life, 1790–1840*. New York: Harper & Row Publishers, 1988.

Long Islander. "Activities of District Attorney A.G. Blue." August 31, 1931, 2.

———. "Alleged Rum Runners Near Smithtown." July 18, 1924, 12.

———. "Amza W. Briggs Dies, Was Former Sheriff, Local Police Chief." August 8, 1957, 1, 4.

———. "Bootleg Gossip." September 7, 1923.

———. "Coast Guards on Way to Funeral Nab Rum Runners." August 7, 1931, 3.

———. "Firemen Do Good Work in Downs Murder Case." May 23, 1924, 3.

———. "Held as Rum Runners." December 14, 1923.

———. "Is Rum Running on the Wane?" April 17, 1925, 14.

———. "More Side Lights on Rum Running." April 17, 1925, 12.

———. "Rum Runners Car Wrecked on Turnpike." January 16, 1925, 13.

———. "Rum Running Still in Progress." January 9, 1925.

Merritt, Jim. "New York's Rum Row." *New York Archives*, Winter 2003. https://www.nysarchivestrust.org/new-york-archives-magazine/magazine-highlights/winter-2003-volume-2-number-3.

Mowry, David. P. "Listening to the Rumrunners: Radio Intelligence during Prohibition." Center for Cryptologic History, 2014. https://www.nsa.gov/about/cryptologic-heritage/historical-figures-publications/publications/pre-wwii/assets/files/rumrunners.pdf.

New York Times. "Crew of Rum Yacht Gets Light Penalty." December 17, 1931, 3.

———. "Dry Men Get *Black Duck*." March 7, 1930, 17.

———. "Held for Fourth Time as Rum-Runner." December 9, 1924, 30.

———. "Jury on Rum Killing Absolves Coast Guard." January 15, 1930, 18.

———. "More Liquor Found on Patrol Boats." January 6, 1930, 1.

———. "$1,000 Bribery Trap Sprung in Suffolk." May 1, 1932, 6.

———. "Policemen Held in Raid." May 13, 1932, 12.

———. "Rum-Runner's Wife Gave Clue for Raid on Broadway Ring: Informed On." September 27, 1925, 1.

———. "Rum Schooner's Crew Found Guilty." April 2, 1925, 12.

———. "Schooner Is Held by Customs Men." January 3, 1925, 6.

———. "Seize Italian Ship as Liquor Suspect." January 2, 1925, 10.

———. "Three Ships Seized as Rum-Runners." February 12, 1925, 12.

———. "To Move Coast Guard Base." 30 August, 1925, 15.

———. "Traps Rum Craft on His First Night." August 7, 1924, 17.

———. "Upholds Coast Guard in *Black Duck* Killing." January 17, 1930, 2.

NicKenzie Lawson, Ellen. *Smugglers, Bootleggers, and Scofflaws: Prohibition and New York City*. Albany: State University of New York Press, 2013.

Okrent, Daniel. *Last Call: The Rise and Fall of Prohibition*. New York: Scribner, 2010.

Patchogue Advance. April 24, 1925, 2.

———. "Big Rum Seizure Is Made in Islip Creek." October 21, 1930, 1, 2.

———. "'Big Shots' of Bootlegging Are Booked for Trial." April 8, 1932, 1, 4.

———. "Blue and Two Officers Fight Pistol Battle in Speeding Cars with Desperate Rum Runners." November 25, 1930, 1, 4.

———. "Bootleg Radios Are Raided by U.S. Men." July 22, 1930, 1, 3.

———. "Brewery in Operation Here Is Raided and Stuff Dumped." June 10, 1930

———. "Catch Two Liquor Loads Same Place Within 12 Hours." December 12, 1930, 1, 2.

———. "Claim Hijackers Gave Raid Tip." April 1, 1927, 1.

———. "Diamond Hookup in This County?" May 5, 1931, 1, 7.

———. "$8000 More Bail on Branding Witnesses." July 17, 1931, 1.

———. "The First of Alleged Torturers Acquitted." November 27, 1931, 1.

———. "Four Patchoguers Are Caught in U.S. Roundup of Island Branch of Big Rum Syndicate." September 9, 1930, 1, 4.

———. "Funeral Brought About Capture of Rum Running Boat." August 4, 1931, 1, 7.

———. "Gustave Fischel Made Mayor of Babylon, Filling Vacancy." June 3, 1932, 4.

———. "Halls at Yaphank and Medford Are Raided by U.S. Dry Officers." May 5, 1931, 1.

———. "Honest Load of Spuds Makes Heavy Job for Doubting Troopers." December 26, 1930, 1.

———. "Judge Condemns the Coast Guard for Its Gun-play." February 21, 1930, 1, 3.

———. "Lack of Tail Light Undoing of Potato-Rum Enterprise." September 30, 1930, 1, 2.

———. "A Magnificent Yacht Caught as a Smuggler." July 3, 1931, 4.

———. "Man and Woman Are Arrested in Bootleg Torture Case." July 10, 1931, 1.

———. "Many Brief Island Notes." September 4, 1931, 1.

———. "Men Were Branded with Hot Irons in Hijacking Feud, They Say." June 30, 1931, 1, 8.

———. "Police Do Battle with Rum Landing Party Here." December 10, 1929, 1, 5.

———. "Police Frustrate Rum Landing Here." December 10, 1929.

———. "Potatoes Used as Blind for Cargo of Contraband Wet Goods Taken in Daylight." April 1, 1930, 1, 4.

———. "Revive Montauk Hijacking Case." December 3, 1926, 5.

———. "Rum Boats Caught." December 30, 1932, 10.

———. "Rum Boats Seized by the Coast Guard." September 23, 1930, 1.

———. "Rum Flows to City in Motor Caravan." March 4, 1930, 1.

———. "Rum Running Outfit Is Seized at Beach." June 3, 1930, 1, 2.

———. "Says Rum Runners Set Up Reign of Terror on River." January 10, 1930, 1,4.

———. "Seize Illegal Radio." May 13, 1932, 5.

———. "Sharp Onslaught Has Given Liquor Runners a Pause." April 15, 1930, 1,5.

———. "Suffolk Votes for Change in Dry Law." September 30, 1930, 1.

———. "Tractor and Trailer Liquor Outfit Seized on Beach." June 1, 1930, 1, 2.

———. "Transfer Load of Rum Right on Main Road?" August 30, 1930, 1.

———. "Two Breweries Are Raided Over Week-end." September 9, 1930, 1, 3.

———. "Two Rum Boats Are Caught off Montauk Point." February 25, 1930, 1, 6.

———. "Two Rum Runners Captured Sunday." December 31 , 1929, 1, 2.

———. "West Sayville Man Sent to Jail for Rum Running with Gang." September 16, 1930, 1.

———. "Wholesale Outbreak of Automobile Stealing." November 1, 1927, 1.

———. "Wilson's Home Linked to Diamond's Case." October 21, 1930, 1, 5.

Pilat, O.R. "Rum Smugglers Use Decoy to Fool Guard." *Brooklyn Daily Eagle*, August 9, 1932, 1.

Port Jefferson Echo. "East Ender to Be Quizzed." October 15, 1921.

———. November 26, 1925, 4.

Port Jefferson Times-Echo. "Crippled Rum Boat Turns Up at Local Yard for Repairs." August 28, 1931, 1.

Rafferty, Pierce. *Scotch on the Rocks.* Performed by Pierce Rafferty. Henry L. Ferguson Museum, Fishers Island, Suffolk County, New York. August 2021.

Rich, Gertrude. *Just Lucky I Guess.* Orient, NY: Privately published, n.d.

———. *A Memoir.* Orient, NY: Privately published, 19??.

Sag Harbor Express. "Guy Fawks [*sic*] Hanged at Round Pond." December 21, 1928, 1.

Singer, Jacqueline. *Prohibition on the Gold Coast of Long Island.* Bloomington, IN: Author House, 2016.

Southampton Express. "Raid Rum Runners at Fort Pond Bay." March 6, 1924, 8.

Southampton Press. "Complaint That Traffic Cop Downs Is Too Severe." May 15, 1924, 4.

———. "First Successful Raid Made on Bootleggers." March 6, 1924, 1.

———. "Four Indicted By Federal Grand Jury." May 24, 1925, 1.

———. "Movie Players Mistaken for Rum Running Crew." January 8, 1925, 3.

———. "Nine Men Drowned at Fire Island Inlet." January 10, 1924, 1.

———. "Rum Running Is Not Yet Dead." April 30, 1925, 1.

———. "Rum Running Not as Profitable as Before." April 10, 1924, 1.

Strobel, Herb, and Richard Wines. Conversation with Amy Kasuga Folk at Hallockville Museum Farm, 2018.

Suffolk County News. "Broere's Bail Fixed at $3,000." April 18, 1930, 1.

———. "Catch Two Rum Boats." February 28, 1930, 1.

———. "Coast Guard Boats Active." January 3, 1930, 1, 8.

———. "Coast Guardsman Is Shot As Rum Shipment Is Seized." May 13, 1932, 1, 3.

———. "Coast Guard Wounded." November 30, 1928, 8.

———. "Contracts Let for Erection of Two New School Buildings in Suffolk." September 18, 1931, 1.

———. "Dist. Atty. and His Men in Gun Fight with Rum Runners." November 28, 1930, 1, 8.

———. "Downs Killed by Rum Runner." May 23, 1924, 1, 8.

———. "Drastic Shakeup in Coast Guard." January 15, 1932, 1, 3.

———. "Find Rum Hoard and Wireless." December 18, 1931, 1, 3.

———. "Five Bodies Recovered." January 11, 1924, 1.

———. "Five Days in Jail for Selling Liquor." April 20, 1928, 10.

———. "Girl Fought Rum Runners." July 27, 1923.

———. "Greenport Woman Exposed Rum Ring." October 2, 1925, 1, 13.

———. "Hazards of Rum Running." November 28, 1924, 1.

———. "Koman Indicted as Rum Briber." April 8, 1932, 1, 8.

———. "Message Washed Ashore." July 16, 1926, 1.

———. "Most Profitable Industry Is Booze." November 14, 1924, 10.

———. "Nab Rum Runner Near Montauk." December 6, 1929, 1, 8.

———. "Nine Drowned on Fire Island Bar." January 4, 1924, 1.

———. "Officer Downs Shot, Killed by Rum Runner." May 22, 1924, 1, 8.

———. "Patchogue." April 24, 1925.

———. "Prohibition Men Now Hunt by Scent." March 14, 1924, 1, 8.

———. "Rum Boat Rammed Off Fire Island." December 19, 1930, 1.

———. "Rum Ship Seized in Fort Pond Bay." January 30, 1931, 1.

———. "Seize 'Bootleg' Sets." July 25, 1930, 1, 8.

———. "Seize Large Load of Liquor." March 14, 1930, 1, 7.

———. "Seize $10,000 Load of Liquor." December 6, 1929, 1, 7.

———. "Seize 2 Truck Loads of Liquor." April 4, 1930, 1, 8.

———. "Spotlight at Last on L.I. Rum Scandal." April 17, 1925, 1, 6.

———. "Spotlight on Long Island Rum Scandal." April 17, 1925, 6.

———. "Swears Officer Was Rum Runner." December 1, 1922.

———. "Thieves Visit Westhampton in Epidemic of Island Robberies." November 20, 1925, 1.

———. "35 Simultaneous Raids." October 18, 1929, 1.

———. "To Investigate Liquor Seizure." December 5, 1930, 1.

———. "Town Talk." December 14, 1923.

———. "West Sayville Boat Is Seized." June 6, 1930, 1, 6.

———. "Why Not Play the Game Fairly?" January 3, 1930, 4.

———. "Wild Waves Saying, 'Yo Ho and a Bottle of Rum.'" April 20, 1927, 6.

Watchman of the Sunrise Trail. "Coast Guard Shot Up Boat." August 27, 1931, 1.

Willoughby, Malcolm F. *Rum War at Sea*. Washington, D.C.: U.S. Government Printing Office, 1964.

ABOUT THE AUTHOR

Author Amy Kasuga Folk is the manager of collections for the Oysterponds Historical Society as well as the manager of collections for the Southold Historical Museum and the Town Historian for Southold. She is also the past president of the Long Island Museum Association and the Region 2 co-chair of the Association of Public Historians. She is the coauthor of several award-winning books focusing on the history of Southold.

Visit us at
www.historypress.com